PRACTICAL COOKERY RECIPES

for HOSPITALITY INTERMEDIATE 1 & 2

Graeme Findlay and George Smith

Photographs by
Suzanne Black

HODDER
GIBSON
AN HACHETTE UK COMPANY

Acknowledgements

To the two Mrs Fs, Anna and Freda, who taught us the basics.

Thanks to Continental Chefs Supplies who kindly donated the plates used to display the food. Thanks also to Jane Cliff and Pat Bacon for providing the nutritional analysis of each recipe.

The Publishers would like to thank the following for permission to reproduce copyright material:

Nutritional analysis by Jane Cliff and Pat Bacon.

All images © Suzanne Black Photography.

Every effort has been made to trace all copyright holders, but if any have been inadvertently overlooked the Publishers will be pleased to make the necessary arrangements at the first opportunity.

Although every effort has been made to ensure that website addresses are correct at time of going to press, Hodder Gibson cannot be held responsible for the content of any website mentioned in this book. It is sometimes possible to find a relocated web page by typing in the address of the home page for a website in the URL window of your browser.

Hachette UK's policy is to use papers that are natural, renewable and recyclable products and made from wood grown in sustainable forests. The logging and manufacturing processes are expected to conform to the environmental regulations of the country of origin.

Orders: please contact Bookpoint Ltd, 130 Milton Park, Abingdon, Oxon OX14 4SB. Telephone: (44) 01235 827720. Fax: (44) 01235 400454. Lines are open 9.00 – 5.00, Monday to Saturday, with a 24-hour message answering service. Visit our website at www.hoddereducation.co.uk. Hodder Gibson can be contacted direct on: Tel: 0141 848 1609; Fax: 0141 889 6315; email: hoddergibson@hodder.co.uk

© Graeme Findlay and George Smith 2010
First published in 2010 by
Hodder Gibson, an imprint of Hodder Education,
An Hachette UK Company
2a Christie Street
Paisley PA1 1NB

Impression number   5 4 3 2 1
Year   2014 2013 2012 2011 2010

Cover photos © Suzanne Black Photography
Typeset in Avenir by DC Graphic Design Limited, Swanley Village, Kent
Printed in Italy

A catalogue record for this title is available from the British Library

ISBN: 978 1444 11072 2

Contents

Introduction

Cooking is not a difficult skill to learn but in life it's a very important one; this book aims to give you the confidence to cook and equip you with the knowledge, understanding and practical experience of basic cookery skills.

These skills will stay with you throughout your life and can be used in the home, helping you to make the correct food choices in order to maintain a healthy diet, and for gaining employment in the Hospitality Industry.

The book contains a selection of uncomplicated recipes that can be served as starters, main course or desserts and they have been written for both two and four portions. Other features in the recipes are

- Key cookery processes and techniques identified

- Tips relating to preparation and serving

- Alternative ingredients that can be used

- Garnishing and service ideas

- Links to current Scottish Qualifications Authority courses

- Nutritional analysis

It is because of national concern with the alarming increase in cases of obesity, particularly with the young, that we invited Jane Cliff and Pat Bacon to develop the nutritional analysis for all of these recipes. Analysis for the nutrients has been performed using the computer software CompEat Pro. Throughout the book, certain assumptions have been made unless stated otherwise: the weight of vegetables refers to prepared weight, chickpeas are cooked and unsalted, all milk is semi-skimmed, oil is vegetable oil.

We've followed a simple method of listing the recipes using three sections: Starters, Main Courses and Desserts, with three sub-sections in each.

To begin with, starters are an important introduction to a meal in that they should stimulate your taste buds with a balance of flavours and textures. Main courses, which provide the main part of a meal, must not dominate it. Care must be taken not to overload a main course dish with either the quantity of food or the flavours used; it's important that after eating a main course dish you don't feel as if you've overeaten. Finally, desserts have the aim of completing your meal and, as such, they should be compiled with that thought in mind. If the dish is too heavy, when using pastry for example, portions can be made that little bit smaller. It's nice to finish your meal with a light dish and we have included many that fall into this category and can be a fitting end to your eating experience.

Whilst the recipes used in the book are tried and tested, care must be taken to follow them in order so you can make each dish to the best of your abilities. The timings that are listed against each dish are there as a guide for you in your planning. You've got to remember that if you're preparing a dish for the first time it will probably take you longer than the recommended time. There will be instances when you will forget to use an ingredient or maybe add one that wasn't listed – this is how professional chefs adapt their recipes so don't worry, carry on cooking and taste the difference. And talking about taste, please make sure that you sample the food you're cooking. It's important for you to understand when food is cooked and one way to do this is by tasting it.

Time will also tell you when food is ready as will the look of it but there's nothing better than sampling what you make in order for you to remember what it tastes like when it's ready. You'll also be able to think back the next time you make the dish, which will be helpful for you to perfect it. As well as working out if the food is cooked, you'll also be able to tell if it needs any salt and pepper added to it. You should always season food to your preferred taste – you have five different types of taste buds on your tongue – bitterness, salty, sour, sweet and Umami, which means tasty or savoury – bearing in mind that we're all different and have our own thoughts on the right or wrong amount of seasoning required depending on our likes/dislikes. Think also of different ways in which to season food – we know that too much salt isn't good for us so try using herbs and spices to flavour food as an alternative.

Being able to cook properly is a life skill that's not difficult to learn and it's actually good fun doing so. When learning how to cook, you'll pick up not only a vast number of skills that you will be able to use in the kitchen, but others such as organisation skills and a knowledge of health and safety legislation that can easily be transferred to many walks of life, be it in the home or when you're working.

We hope that you enjoy using this book: take care with it, and make sure you keep it in a safe place as we're sure you'll use it often as you pick up skills and develop your own individual cooking style.

CHAPTER 1

Basic knowledge

The following areas are important basic skills that you must have an understanding of to be able to work efficiently in a kitchen.

Hygiene, health and safety in the kitchen

Safe practices should be adopted at all times when working in a kitchen environment, with importance placed on personal as well as kitchen hygiene. Opportunities must be taken to integrate food hygiene and health and safety knowledge when taking part in kitchen activities. By doing so, it will become second nature and you'll understand and remember their importance more easily.

The kitchen can be a dangerous place if those working in it do not have a basic understanding of how to go about their work in a sensible manner.

Personal hygiene

In order to be able to operate effectively in the kitchen, it's important that you're aware of the need to observe the highest possible standards of personal hygiene. This is important so as to give the correct image to the public, protect the food you are working with and to ensure that you are carrying out your work legally.

Aspects of personal hygiene that you must be aware of and carry out are:

- Wear the correct, clean protective clothing – chefs nowadays wear a vast array of colours as well as the traditional white and the clothing's function is to protect them from the heat and the food from contamination.
- Wash your hands before and after handling foods.
- Take care of your finger nails – keep them short, clean and varnish free.
- Cover cuts and boils to avoid the spread of infection.
- Do not wear jewellery unless permitted.
- Keep your hair tied back if it's long.
- If you are suffering from a cold/sneezing, avoid coming into contact with foods.

Kitchen hygiene

Another important area of food safety is kitchen hygiene and these are basic areas which it's useful to have a working knowledge of:

- Cleaning and disinfection – remove dirt, disinfect equipment and surfaces. Adopt a clean-as-you-go way of working.
- How to prevent the contamination of food – harmful bacteria can be transferred from yourself, from an object or from other food.
- Waste disposal of food – dispose of food correctly, taking into consideration the rules of the kitchen you are working in and current environmental issues.
- Food storage – store raw and cooked meat, fish and dairy products in a refrigerator at a temperature of between 0 °C and 40 °C – the

golden rule is that raw food must not be stored above cooked food as juices from the raw food may fall onto the cooked food and contaminate it. Dried and canned foods and fresh fruit and vegetables should be stored in a dry, cool, well-ventilated area.

- Hazard analysis – it's important that you understand where problems may arise, from the receiving of goods to the service of customers. At certain stages of the storage and production of foods, contamination may occur and this possibility must be eliminated. Please be aware at all times of the correct storage requirements depending on the process you are carrying out in order to eliminate the risk to your customers.

Health and safety

It's very important that when you're preparing, cooking and serving food you're aware of the risks that are involved and try to avoid them. The best way to become aware of what accidents can occur is to undertake training in health and safety. The following list of safe working practices will help you begin to understand:

- Turn off all appliances when not in use.
- Do not attempt to move pots etc. over naked flames/hot rings.
- Do not leave pot handles over naked flames/hot rings or protruding over the edge of the cooker.
- Do not leave small equipment (wooden/metal spoon) in pots whilst cooking food in them.
- Do not use a damp cloth to lift hot items of equipment.
- If carrying a knife, make sure the point is towards the floor.
- Do not catch a falling knife.
- Use a chopping board to cut food on, never the table or in your hand.
- Secure your chopping board with rubber matting before use.
- Have one item for chopping on the chopping board at a time.

- Clean up any spillages immediately.
- Don't carry hot/heavy goods on your own.
- Dispose of waste packaging correctly.
- Don't obstruct fire exits, corridors or stairways.
- Follow instructions on cleaning materials.
- Keep chemicals away from food.
- Report all accidents that occur.
- And finally, make sure that you know where the first aid box is located.

Carrying out your work

When carrying out your work, emphasis must be placed on the following:

- Wearing the correct clean, protective clothing.
- Making sure that you have the exact food items/quantities to produce the dishes you have planned.
- Gathering all equipment, both preparation and serving, prior to starting to cook.
- Keeping your work area clean at all times – adopt a 'clean-as-you-go' attitude.
- Using equipment correctly and in a safe manner. For example, don't forget about food you have placed in the oven or covered in a pot with a lid.
- Keeping as near as is possible to the times that you have planned.
- Presenting food to a commercially acceptable standard.

Planning

Being organised is an excellent skill to have and when you've mastered the basics of it, e.g. meeting deadlines you've set in a plan, it's a skill that you can transfer to any job you do.

When cooking, being organised and knowing when to carry out your work is very important. In the kitchen you will need to be able to work methodically and at a controlled pace, follow a recipe or recipes and carry this out in a clean and efficient manner. Our advice is that you clean-as-you-go; by doing so this will reduce the risk of contaminating the food you are working with and ensure that you are free of obstacles in your work area. Carrying out your work efficiently and to plan will mean that you'll be using less energy, both physical and mechanical.

Good planning starts with reading and understanding the recipes that you plan to cook. From there, you will be able to collect the ingredients and necessary equipment required to carry out the production and service of the dishes. As a guide, the following points will be helpful for this process:

- Read the recipes and organise the tasks within them.

- Work out when your food has to be served and produce a time plan that you can follow.

- Gather all your ingredients into containers for each dish.

- Set aside the equipment you'll need for cooking, holding and serving the food.

- Visualise how you would like to serve each dish, thinking about finishing and decorating skills.

By carrying out the planning, weighing and measuring of your dishes, you will develop aspects of the core skills of problem solving and numeracy. You will further develop these very useful, transferable skills as you prepare the different dishes in this book.

As a guide to help you with the planning of your work, we have produced examples of work plans using the following recipes – Smoked bacon melts (page 33) and Leek flan (page 71) for a two-dish, 1½ hour session and Butternut squash soup (page 39), Chicken burger with relish (page 55) and Chocolate tart (page 92) for a three-dish, 2½ hour session. These can be found in Appendices 1 and 2 on pages 118–119. One way to further enhance your plan of work is to photocopy each dish on different coloured paper. You could then cut each step of the dishes out and reassemble them in the logical order that you see them being carried out. As each dish will be colour-coded, it will be very easy to understand what stage you are at in the production of each one.

Conversion charts

In order to avoid confusion, the ingredients in the recipes are all listed in grammes (g) or millilitres (ml). Measuring the large grammes (g) amounts is easy enough using scales; however, for the smaller amounts listed as millilitres (ml), we used measuring spoons.

As there are many different types of ovens available, we have given each required temperature – Fahrenheit (F), Celsius (C) and gas mark – in the recipes.

Spoon measures

1.25 ml	=	¼ teaspoon
2.50 ml	=	½ teaspoon
5 ml	=	1 teaspoon
10 ml	=	1 dessertspoon
15 ml	=	1 tablespoon
20 ml	=	4 teaspoons

Oven temperature

	Gas mark	°C	°F
	¼	115	240
	½	120	250
cool	1	135	275
	2	150	300
warm	3	160	325
	4	175	350
hot	5	190	375
	6	200	400
very hot	7	215	425
	8	230	450
	9	245	475

CHAPTER 2

Starters

1 Cullen skink

Preparation and cooking time – 30 minutes

2 portions	4 portions	Ingredients
½	1	onion, small
½	1	celery stick
30 g	60 g	butter
120 g	240 g	potatoes
150 ml	300 ml	fish stock
120 g	240 g	smoked haddock
200 ml	400 ml	milk
		black pepper
15 ml	30 ml	parsley, chopped
15 ml	30 ml	double cream

1. Chop the onion and celery finely.

2. Melt the butter in a large pan, add the onion and celery and sweat for 2 minutes.

3. Cut the potatoes into small dice and add to the pan, cooking for a further 1 minute.

4. Add the stock, bring to the boil and then simmer for 10–15 minutes.

5. Cut the haddock into even sized dice and add to the pan with the milk and black pepper.

6. Simmer for 5 minutes and test for seasoning.

7. Finish with the parsley and cream and serve.

Energy	303 kcal
Fat	18.63 g / 11.45 g saturated
Carbohydrate	18.4 g / 7.56 g sugar
Protein	16.8 g
Fibre	1.4 g

Key cookery processes and techniques
Chopping/sweating/dicing/boiling/simmering

Tips
The potatoes and fish could be chopped into macedoine and the celery for brunoise. This would allow for opportunities to develop skills. Alternatively the soup could be liquidised giving another preparation technique to the dish; there would be no need to cut the vegetables so precisely, and it would be suitable for Intermediate 1 level, also taking less time to make.

Alternative ways in which to enhance the dish
If you change the fish for leek, this can give you a vegetarian alternative. The cream can be replaced with half-fat crème fraîche and the milk with semi-skimmed to give you a healthier option. You can also substitute chives for the parsley to give a different taste.

Ideas for garnishing
Serve this soup with oatcakes or crusty wholemeal bread. If you have enough time, a savoury herb scone/bread roll would not only complement the soup but would also give a balance of skills in this recipe.

Links to the content of following courses
Hospitality Practical Cookery Int2/Hospitality Skills for Work Int2/Hospitality General Operations Int2

Chilli salmon patties with lime dressing

Preparation and cooking time – 45 minutes

2 portions	4 portions	Ingredients
½	1	onion
½	1	red chilli
1	2	garlic cloves
½ cm	1 cm	ginger root
25 ml	50 ml	oil
200 g	400 g	chickpeas, cooked
10 ml	20 ml	coriander, chopped
125 g	250 g	salmon, cooked
½	1	egg
½	1	lime
100 ml	200 ml	mayonnaise
10 ml	20 ml	parsley, chopped
		seasoning

1. Finely chop the onion, chilli, garlic and ginger.

2. Heat half the oil in a pan and sweat the mixture until soft.

3. Blend the chickpeas, onion mix, chopped coriander and salmon. Add the egg, season and chill for 15 minutes.

4. For the dressing, remove the zest from the lime, chop and add to the mayonnaise. Add the parsley and adjust consistency/taste with lime juice if required. Chill until required.

6. Shape the patties into rounds and chill for a further 15 minutes.

7. Heat the remaining oil in a shallow frying pan and fry the patties until golden brown. Remove from the pan onto kitchen paper and season lightly.

8. Serve with the lime dressing and accompaniments of your choice.

Energy	704 kcal
Fat	57.85 g / 8.45 g saturated
Carbohydrate	20.8 g / 3.86 g sugar
Protein	26.6 g
Fibre	5.0 g

Key cookery processes and techniques
Chopping/mixing/sweating/blending/shaping/shallow frying

Tips
If the mixture is too wet, add some breadcrumbs to stiffen it up. When shaping your patties use a palette knife and the bottom of your palm/little finger to help get the shape you want. Alternatively, you could shape them using a round cutter. Resist the temptation to keep turning your patties whilst they are frying as extra movement will cause them to break up.

Alternative ways in which to enhance the dish
The patties could be coated in breadcrumbs to give a different texture/finish to them. Other fish can be used as well as or instead of salmon. For a vegetarian option, omit the fish altogether and add the same weight of cooked vegetables.

Ideas for garnishing
The dish could be finished with a nice seasonal salad of your choice, bound with a sweet chilli jam.

Links to the content of following courses
Hospitality Practical Cookery Int2/Hospitality Skills for Work Int2/Hospitality General Operations Int2

3 Crab wraps with mango salsa

Preparation and cooking time – 25 minutes

2 portions	4 portions	Ingredients
¼	½	red chilli
½	1	shallot
1	2	coriander, sprigs
150 g	300 g	crab meat
5 ml	10 ml	grain mustard
45 ml	90 ml	mayonnaise
squeeze		lemon juice
		seasoning
¼	½	Chinese lettuce
Salsa		
½	1	red chilli
½	1	red onion
½	1	lime, zest and juice
½	1	mango
7.5 ml	15 ml	sesame oil
7.5 ml	15 ml	olive oil
few		chopped mint leaves

1. Finely dice the chilli and shallot and chop the coriander.

2. Mix with the crab meat, mustard and mayonnaise.

3. Season with the lemon juice, salt and pepper.

4. Separate the lettuce leaves and cut into 12 cm wide strips.

5. Flatten the leaves carefully and spoon the filling along one end. Roll up, secure neatly and chill until required.

6. For the salsa, finely chop the red chilli and red onion and dice the mango. Mix with the remaining ingredients, season and reserve.

7. To serve: cut wraps in half, arrange on a plate with salsa.

Key cookery processes and techniques
Dicing/chopping/mixing

Tips
The Salsa can be stored in the refrigerator for 2–3 days for future use. Use a buffet skewer or cocktail stick to help secure the roll.

Alternative ways in which to enhance the dish
The crab can be replaced with tuna to make the dish less expensive. Tortilla wraps can be used instead of lettuce leaves.

Ideas for garnishing
You could use some thinned down mayonnaise to decorate the plate and give a contrast to the colours already there.

Links to the content of following courses
Hospitality Practical Cookery Int1/Hospitality Skills for Work Int1/Home Economics Standard Grade

Energy	364 kcal
Fat	29.13 g / 4.23 g saturated
Carbohydrate	9.9 g / 8.71 g sugar
Protein	16.2 g
Fibre	1.8 g

4 Tuna Niçoise salad

Preparation and cooking time – 40 minutes

2 portions	4 portions	Ingredients
100 g	200 g	baby new potatoes
2	4	eggs
100 g	200 g	French beans
4	8	cherry tomatoes
100 g	200 g	tuna, canned
10 g	20 g	parsley
15 ml	30 ml	olive oil
5 ml	10 ml	lemon juice

1. Wash the new potatoes before placing in a pan with seasoned cold water.

2. Bring to the boil and simmer for 20–25 minutes, drain, cool and drain again. Reserve for later.

3. Cover the eggs with cold, seasoned water in a pan. Bring to the boil and simmer for 12 minutes. Refresh under cold water, peel and reserve for later.

4. Top and tail the French beans. Plunge into rapidly boiling, seasoned water for 2 minutes. Remove immediately and plunge into ice cold water. Reserve.

5. Wash, dry and quarter the cherry tomatoes.

6. Drain the tinned tuna and leave the fish in large chunks.

7. Wash, dry and chop the parsley.

8. Quarter the eggs or slice into five pieces.

9. Cut the French beans in half and slice the potatoes into 1 cm slices.

10. Place the oil and lemon juice into a bowl and season lightly.

11. Carefully mix all the ingredients into the dressing and serve in a cold salad bowl or plate.

Key cookery processes and techniques
Boiling/simmering/draining/refreshing/peeling/blanching/slicing/mixing

Tips
This is a great dish for beginners. The potatoes and eggs could all be pre-cooked which would allow additional time to concentrate on the slicing and chopping of the ingredients. If a plum or beef tomato is used, it's advisable to blanch the tomato to remove the skin and make it easier to slice and to enhance the skills required for the preparation of this dish.

Alternative ways in which to enhance the dish
The boiled egg could be poached to give an additional technique to the dish. The cherry tomatoes could be replaced by plum, vine or even sun dried. There is also the opportunity to remove the tuna making the salad vegetarian.

Ideas for garnishing
Crusty wholemeal bread, black olives, anchovies and salad leaves such as endive or bib lettuce can all be used as possible garnishes for this classic French salad. Although the salad is better served with the ingredients mixed together, the individual ingredients could be coated with the dressing and laid artistically onto the plate allowing customers to select their own desired composition while dining. Parmesan cheese freshly shaved on top of the salad is a good way to finish this dish.

Links to the content of following courses
Hospitality Practical Cookery Int1/Hospitality Skills for Work Int1/Home Economics Standard Grade

Energy	261 kcal
Fat	14.9 g / 3.19 g saturated
Carbohydrate	10.7 g / 2.86 g sugar
Protein	21.7 g
Fibre	2.2 g

Kedgeree

Preparation and cooking time – 55 minutes

2 portions	4 portions	Ingredients
½	1	egg
45 g	90 g	basmati rice
150 g	300 g	smoked haddock fillet
½	1	bay leaf
½ cm	1 cm	ginger root, peeled
2	4	spring onions
½	1	garlic clove
1	2	tomatoes
25 g	50 g	butter
10 g	20 g	curry powder
½	1	lemon, juice
5 ml	10 ml	chopped parsley

Energy	289 kcal
Fat	13.96 g / 7.33 g saturated
Carbohydrate	23.1 g / 2.24 g sugar
Protein	19.2 g
Fibre	2.0 g

1. Boil the egg for 10 minutes then cool under running water.

2. While the egg is cooking, boil the rice in a separate pan for 10–12 minutes until the grains are just tender and refresh under running cold water. Allow to drain.

3. In a shallow saucepan, barely cover the haddock with water, add the bay leaf and poach for 5 minutes. Allow the fish to cool in the liquid then flake into large chunks and reserve for later.

4. Grate the ginger; chop the spring onion and garlic and dice the tomato.

5. Melt the butter in a pan, add the ginger, spring onion and garlic and sweat for 3 minutes on a gentle heat with a tight fitting lid.

6. Add the curry powder and cook for a further 2–3 minutes.

7. Add the chopped tomatoes and lemon juice.

8. Peel and quarter the boiled egg.

9. Add the rice and fish to the curry pan and gently warm through.

10. When warm add the egg and parsley and gently fork through. Taste and season if required.

11. Serve on a warm plate.

Key cookery processes and techniques
Boiling/poaching/grating/chopping/dicing/sweating/peeling

Tips
Using pre-cooked rice and eggs will cut down on the preparation time for this dish. The spring onion and ginger can be finely chopped but for additional skills try to brunoise these. The tomato should be prepared as follows:

1. Remove the eye of the tomato.

2. Plunge into ample, boiling water for 10 seconds.

3. Immediately remove and place into ice cold water.

4. Remove the skin.

5. Cut into quarters.

6. Cut the seeds out and dice the flesh.

Alternative ways in which to enhance the dish
Although it is preferred that smoked fish is used for this dish other fish can be used, including shellfish such as mussels or prawns. Chicken can also be an alternative or even an addition to the specified recipe.

Ideas for garnishing
A mild curry sauce can be served in a sauce boat. As this dish is popular at breakfast time, a soft poached egg served on top is a nice accompaniment. Alternatively the kedgeree could be served as part of a poached chicken or smoked haddock meal for brunch.

Links to the content of following courses
Hospitality Practical Cookery Int1/Hospitality Skills for Work Int1/Home Economics Standard Grade

Salmon fish cakes with watercress and grapefruit salad

Preparation and cooking time – 60 minutes

2 portions	4 portions	Ingredients
25 g	50 g	celery
25 g	50 g	leek
5 g	10 g	butter
150 g	300 g	salmon
5 g	10 g	chives
5 g	10 g	parsley
50 ml	100 ml	mayonnaise
1 drop	2 drops	tabasco sauce
100 g	200 g	breadcrumbs
		seasoning
50 g	100 g	flour
200 ml	400 ml	milk
½	1	egg
		oil for frying
Salad		
½	1	grapefruit
20 g	40 g	watercress
1	2	radish
15 ml	30 ml	olive oil

Fishcakes

1. Preheat the oven to 180 °C/360 °F/gas mark 4.

2. Dice the celery and leek.

3. Melt the butter in a pan with a tight fitting lid and, over a medium heat, add the celery and leek. Lightly season and sweat for 1–2 minutes until slightly soft/no colour, then tip into a bowl.

4. Dice the salmon and chop the chives and parsley.

5. Add the fish to the bowl along with the mayonnaise, chives, parsley, tabasco and 60 g/ 125g of the breadcrumbs, season with salt and freshly ground pepper, mix together and shape into cakes, one per portion.

6. Organise three trays: one with flour, one with egg wash (mix the egg and milk together) and one with breadcrumbs. Coat each fish cake first in flour, dip in egg wash and finally coat in breadcrumbs, reshape the cakes and place in the fridge to firm up.

7. Heat the oil in a frying pan over a medium high heat and fry the fish cakes until crisp on each side, transfer to a tray and place in the oven for 5–6 minutes until cooked through.

Salad

1. Peel and segment the grapefruit, reserving the juice.

2. Trim the watercress, removing the thick stalks.

3. Slice the radish thinly.

4. Make a dressing with the olive oil and reserved grapefruit juice.

5. Toss through the salad ingredients and season lightly.

To serve

Arrange the salad on a plate then place the fish cakes at the side.

Energy	661 kcal
Fat	41.16 g / 8.3 g saturated
Carbohydrate	48.6 g / 10.62 g sugar
Protein	27.2 g
Fibre	2.9 g

Key cookery processes and techniques
Dicing/sweating/chopping/mixing/shaping/
coating/shallow frying/baking/segmenting

Tips
The fish cakes could be made the day before and
refrigerated. The following day they could be
coated and then cooked. For Intermediate 2
candidates try to dice the vegetables into brunoise
and chop the parsley very finely. Make sure that
the fish cakes are divided and shaped so they are
the same size. While the fish cakes are in the
fridge firming up, the salad can be prepared as
long as the watercress is not dressed until service
as it will wilt.

Alternative ways in which to enhance the dish
Other salad leaves could be used such as rocket or
frizzy. If grapefruits are not available then other
citrus fruits could be used, e.g. limes or lemons,
which would complement the fish. Prawn, crab or
smoked haddock could be used or even a
combination of them all. Use cooked chicken instead
of salmon as an alternative to fish.

Ideas for garnishing
Serve with a dill and lemon mayonnaise or a lime
and caper oil based dressing. With the addition of
tabasco in the fish cake, a sweet chilli sauce would
complement the dish.

Links to the content of following courses
Hospitality Practical Cookery Int2/Hospitality Skills
for Work Int2/Hospitality General Operations Int2

 # Salmon and sweet potato broth

Preparation and cooking time – 45 minutes

2 portions	4 portions	Ingredients
50 g	100 g	short pasta
½	1	onion, small
1	2	garlic cloves
½	1	red chilli
175 g	350 g	sweet potato
30 ml	60 ml	oil
500 ml	1 l	vegetable stock
150 g	300 g	salmon, diced
50 g	100 g	spinach

1. Add the pasta to a pan of boiling, lightly seasoned water and cook for 12–15 minutes.

2. Drain when ready and reserve.

3. Finely dice the onion, garlic and chilli.

4. Cut the sweet potato into small dice.

5. Heat the oil in a large pan and add the garlic and onion; sweat with a tight fitting lid on the pan for 2–3 minutes until soft.

6. Stir in the chilli and sweet potatoes, gently mix and season lightly.

7. Add the stock and cook very gently for 5 minutes.

8. Add the salmon to the stock and cook gently for a further 5 minutes.

9. Wash and cut the spinach into strips.

10. Finish the soup by adding the spinach and pasta, taste for seasoning, bring back to the boil and serve.

Energy	450 kcal
Fat	24.2 g / 3.36 g saturated
Carbohydrate	40.1 g / 7.49 g sugar
Protein	20.3 g
Fibre	3.7 g

Key cookery processes and techniques
Boiling/dicing/sweating/mixing

Tips
When adding the pasta to the pan of boiling water stir in gently; this will stop it sticking together as it starts to soften/cook.

Alternative ways in which to enhance the dish
Try using different pastas such as 2 cm length spaghetti, penne or noodles. The sweet potatoes could be replaced by potatoes.

Ideas for garnishing
Serve with freshly sliced wholemeal or granary bread. Also a sesame toasted crostini: sliced baguette, brushed with sesame oil and sesame seeds, then lightly toasted.

Links to the content of following courses
Hospitality Practical Cookery Int1/Hospitality Skills for Work Int1/Home Economics Standard Grade

Tuna broccoli quiche

Preparation and cooking time – 45 minutes

2 portions	4 portions	Ingredients
25 g	50 g	plain flour
15 g	30 g	wholemeal flour
pinch		salt
20 g	40 g	margarine
10 ml	15/20 ml	water
1	2	eggs
37.5 ml	75 ml	milk
12.5 ml	25 ml	mayonnaise
10 g	20 g	mustard
100 g	200 g	canned tuna, drained
25 g	50 g	broccoli, cooked
10 g	20 g	Cheddar cheese, grated

1. Preheat the oven to 180 °C/360 °F gas mark 4.

2. Sieve the flours and the pinch of salt into a large bowl then add the grains from the sieve.

3. Rub in the margarine until the mixture resembles breadcrumbs.

4. Add enough water and knead carefully to make a smooth pastry.

5. Roll the pastry, line the flan ring then leave to rest.

6. Beat eggs, milk, mayonnaise and mustard together.

7. Put tuna and broccoli into unbaked pie shell.

8. Pour egg and milk mixture over the tuna and broccoli.

9. Sprinkle on the grated cheese over all.

10. Bake for 25 minutes or until set.

Energy	242 kcal
Fat	13.51 g / 3.2 g saturated
Carbohydrate	15.2 g / 0.93 g sugar
Protein	16.0 g
Fibre	1.4 g

Key cookery processes and techniques
Sieving/rubbing-in/kneading/rolling/lining/beating/grating/baking

Tips
Take care not to overwork the pastry as it will become dry and difficult to roll out. Roll out to a thickness of 3–5 mm to ensure even cooking. Pass the egg mixture through a sieve prior to adding it to the pastry case to remove the 'white' chalazae (the bit that suspends the yolk in the raw egg).

Alternative ways in which to enhance the dish
The tuna can be replaced with vegetables of the same weight to give a vegetarian alternative. The mayonnaise can be replaced with fromage frais to give a healthier option. Add thinly sliced tomatoes to the top of the quiche before you sprinkle with the cheese to give a contrasting colour/finish. You could prepare individual quiches instead of one large one.

Ideas for garnishing
When serving, a salad of rocket leaves, chives and dill would complement the flavours in the quiche along with a herb mayonnaise.

Links to the content of following courses
Hospitality Practical Cookery Int2/Hospitality Skills for Work Int2/Hospitality General Operations Int2

Fish-based starters

9 Savoury smoked fish flan

Preparation and cooking time – 60 minutes

2 portions	4 portions	Ingredients
25 g	50 g	plain flour
15 g	30 g	wholemeal flour
20 g	40 g	margarine
10 ml	15/20 ml	water
10 g	20 g	shallot
25 g	50 g	leek
40 g	75 g	smoked fish, undyed
5 g	10 g	butter
5 g	10 g	chives, freshly snipped
15 g	25 g	Cheddar cheese, grated
1	2	eggs
25 ml	50 ml	milk
25 ml	50 ml	whipping cream

Energy	243 kcal
Fat	15.26 g / 8.26 g saturated
Carbohydrate	15.5 g / 1.35 g sugar
Protein	11.9 g
Fibre	1.1 g

1. Preheat the oven to 180 °C/360 °F gas mark 4.
2. Sieve the flours and a pinch of salt into a large bowl then add the grains from the sieve.
3. Rub in the margarine until the mixture resembles breadcrumbs.
4. Add enough water and knead carefully to make a smooth pastry.
5. Roll the pastry, line the flan ring then leave to rest.
6. Prick the pastry base then line with foil and baking beans and bake blind for 15 minutes.
7. Wash the shallot and the leek and pat dry.
8. Dice the shallot and julienne the leek.
9. Dice fish into ½ cm sized pieces.
10. Sweat the shallots and the leek in a little butter, season lightly.
11. Remove the beans and foil, then spread the shallot mixture evenly on the base of the baked pastry case.
12. Spread the diced fish evenly over the shallot mixture.
13. Sprinkle the chives evenly over the fish and top with grated cheese.
14. Beat the egg, milk and cream together, pour into a jug, then fill the flan with the mixture.
15. Bake for 15–20 minutes until set and golden in colour.
16. Remove and allow to rest on a cooling tray prior to serving.

Key cookery processes and techniques
Sieving/rubbing in/kneading/rolling/baking blind/
dicing/julienne/sweating/baking

Tips
Try making the pastry and preparing the filling the
day before and finishing the flan the next day. If
you have enough time you could always sweat the
vegetables off as well the day before.

Alternative ways in which to enhance the dish
Use shrimps or large prawns instead of or as well as
some of the smoked fish. You could also use all
milk instead of the cream to make the dish
healthier.

Ideas for garnishing
Accompany with freshly prepared salad of rocket,
tomato and onion dressed and seasoned just before
serving. A little lemon flavoured mayonnaise would
also go well with this dish.

Links to the content of following courses
Hospitality Practical Cookery Int2/Hospitality
Skills for Work Int2/Hospitality General Operations
Int2

10 Ginger fish veloute

Preparation and cooking time – 45 minutes

2 portions	4 portions	Ingredients
1	2	shallots
50 g	100 g	celery
25 g	50 g	leek
1 cm	2 cm	ginger root, peeled
25 g	50 g	butter
25 g	50 g	flour
200 ml	400 ml	fish stock
50 ml	100 ml	cream
		seasoning

1. Slice the shallot into rings and the celery and leek into even sized pieces.

2. Roughly grate the ginger root.

3. Sweat the shallot, celery, leek and ginger in the butter.

4. Mix the flour in well, cook for 2 minutes, making sure the mixture does not stick to the bottom of the pan, then remove from the heat.

5. Add the fish stock gradually, stirring well to avoid any lumps. Bring to the boil, stirring continuously, then turn down the heat.

6. Cook out for 15 minutes and remove from the heat.

7. Blend and pass the soup into a clean pan.

8. Bring back to the boil, add the cream and season to taste.

Energy	201 kcal
Fat	15.4 g / 9.59 g saturated
Carbohydrate	13.7 g / 3.27 g sugar
Protein	2.8 g
Fibre	1.4 g

Key cookery processes and techniques
Chopping/grating/sweating/stirring/blending/boiling

Tips
'Veloute' means 'velvet' – to ensure a nice, smooth velvety consistency and even cooking, mix the flour in well so as to avoid any lumps.

Alternative ways in which to enhance the dish
Add some cooked fish of your choice to the soup prior to serving to give a contrast in texture and flavour.

Ideas for garnishing
Save some of the cream and use to pour onto the soup prior to serving. A little chopped dill will complement the fish and helps to give colour and flavour.

Links to the content of following courses
Hospitality Practical Cookery Int1/Hospitality Skills for Work Int1/Home Economics Standard Grade

1 Tuscan bean and sausage soup

Preparation and cooking time – 50 minutes

2 portions	4 portions	Ingredients
100 g	200 g	Italian sausage
½	1	red onion, small
1	2	carrots
1	2	celery sticks
1	2	garlic cloves
200 g	400 g	tomatoes, tinned chopped
7.5 ml	15 ml	tomato paste
300 ml	600 ml	vegetable stock seasoning
200 g	400 g	beans, cooked mixed

1. Cut the sausage into small, even sized pieces.

2. Heat a large non-stick saucepan and gently shallow fry the sausage, during which time the fat will melt to produce an oil.

3. Cut the onion, carrot and celery into a small dice and crush the garlic.

4. Remove the sausage from the pan onto kitchen paper and reserve.

5. Add the onion to the pan and sauté for about 5 minutes or until soft.

6. Stir in the garlic, carrot and celery and continue to cook for a further 5 minutes.

7. Add the tomatoes, tomato paste, stock and seasoning.

8. Bring to the boil, reduce to a simmer and cook for 20–30 minutes or until the vegetables are soft.

9. Place half of the vegetable mixture into a food processor and blend until smooth, then return to the pan.

10. Add the beans and sausage, bring to the boil and season to taste.

Key cookery processes and techniques
Cutting/shallow frying/dicing/sautéing/simmering/blending

Tips
Take care not to over colour the sausage as this will flavour the soup.

Alternative ways in which to enhance the dish
Try serving the soup without blending it for a chunkier texture. Blanche the tomatoes and dice the flesh of the tomato to add additional skills to the preparation and give the dish a nicer finish.

Ideas for garnishing
Finish the soup with some green pesto – this adds a beautiful, contrasting colour and of course gives a lovely taste of basil. You could also try making herb croutons by simply mixing toasted croutons with pesto oil.

Links to the content of following courses
Hospitality Practical Cookery Int1/Hospitality Skills for Work Int1/Home Economics Standard Grade

Energy	237 kcal
Fat	11.99 g / 4.87 g saturated
Carbohydrate	18.7 g / 9.64 g sugar
Protein	14.5 g
Fibre	4.5 g

2 Baked stuffed tomato with a salami crust

Preparation and cooking time – 50 minutes

2 portions	4 portions	Ingredients
2	4	beef tomatoes, ripe
1	2	salami slices, large
7.5 ml	15 ml	olive oil
½	1	garlic clove, crushed
25 g	50 g	breadcrumbs, fresh
25 g	50 g	mascarpone cheese
75 g	125 g	ricotta cheese
15 ml	30 ml	basil leaves, finely chopped
		seasoning

1. Cut each tomato in half horizontally, scoop out the insides and discard.

2. Sprinkle the tomato halves with salt and drain upside down for 30 minutes.

3. Preheat the oven to 220 °C/425 °F/gas mark 7.

4. Cut the salami into a small dice.

5. Heat the olive oil in a pan, add the salami and garlic and cook for 30 seconds.

6. Stir in the breadcrumbs and cook for 2 minutes.

7. Mix together the mascarpone, ricotta and basil, and season with black pepper.

8. Wash the tomatoes to remove any excess salt and pat dry.

9. Fill each tomato with the cheese mixture and top with the breadcrumb mixture.

10. Transfer the tomatoes to a baking tray and bake for 15–20 minutes, or until they are slightly blistered and the tops are golden.

Key cookery processes and techniques
Cutting/dicing/shallow frying/mixing/filling/baking

Tips
When draining the tomatoes, place them on a cooling rack over a tray. Take care not to over colour the salami and garlic as this will give a bitter flavour.

Alternative ways in which to enhance the dish
The salami can be removed from the crust to give a vegetarian alternative, add a little paprika to give a similar flavour. Add chopped parsley to the crust mixture to give a nice colour and flavour.

Ideas for garnishing
Sprigs of herbs and rocket are the ideal way in which to garnish this dish – the flavours of basil or marjoram go well with tomato.

Links to the content of following courses
Hospitality Practical Cookery Int/Hospitality Skills for Work Int/Home Economics Standard Grade

Energy	229 kcal
Fat	15.51 g / 7.33 g saturated
Carbohydrate	15.9 g / 6.22 g sugar
Protein	7.3 g
Fibre	1.8 g

Mexican chowder

Preparation and cooking time – 40 minutes

2 portions	4 portions	Ingredients
75 g	150 g	chicken breast meat, skinless
20 g	40 g	onion
½	1	garlic clove
½	1	green chilli
½	1	tomato
10 g	20 g	butter
500 ml	1 l	chicken stock
1 g	2 g	ground cumin
50 ml	100 ml	cream
25 g	50 g	white Cheddar cheese, grated
100 g	200 g	sweetcorn
dash		hot pepper sauce
		fresh coriander, for garnish
		seasoning

1. Cut the chicken into 1–2 cm dice, the onion into a fine dice, crush the garlic, finely chop the chilli and dice the tomato.

2. Heat the butter in a pan, add the chicken, seal and remove.

3. Add the onion and garlic and sweat for 5 minutes to soften.

4. Pour the stock into the pot and add the cumin.

5. Bring to a boil, reduce to a low heat, cover and simmer for 5 minutes.

6. Stir in the chicken, chilli, cream, cheese, sweetcorn and hot pepper sauce.

7. Cook, stirring frequently, until the cheese is melted.

8. Stir in the diced tomato and season to taste.

9. Garnish with chopped coriander and serve.

Key cookery processes and techniques
Cutting/dicing/chopping/shallow frying/sweating/simmering/stirring

Tips
After adding the cheese, take care not to boil the soup as this will make the cheese go stringy and the soup greasy.

Alternative ways in which to enhance the dish
Add shellfish of your choice to give a different flavour or if you don't want to use chicken, use fish instead.

Ideas for garnishing
Cut tortillas into strips, sprinkle with some chilli oil and crisp up in the oven to make a nice accompaniment for the soup. Serving with a tabasco sauce would allow diners to vary how hot and spicy this soup was.

Links to the content of following courses
Hospitality Practical Cookery Int2/Hospitality Skills for Work Int2/Hospitality General Operations Int2

Energy	491 kcal
Fat	32.01 g / 18.48 g saturated
Carbohydrate	21.6 g / 5.76 g sugar
Protein	30.9 g
Fibre	2.2 g

4 Chicken salad Caesar style

Preparation and cooking time – 40 minutes

2 portions	4 portions	Ingredients
½	1	ciabatta, medium
15 ml	30 ml	olive oil
1	2	chicken breast, skinless
½	1	garlic clove
30 ml	60 ml	mayonnaise
7.5 ml	15 ml	white wine vinegar
12.5 g	25 g	parmesan cheese
½	1	cos lettuce
8	16	chive strips
		seasoning

Energy	422 kcal
Fat	23.77 g / 4.55 g saturated
Carbohydrate	27.3 g / 2.69 g sugar
Protein	26.1 g
Fibre	1.8 g

1. Heat the oven to 200 °C/400 °F/gas mark 6.
2. Cut the ciabatta bread into large croutons.
3. Spread over a large baking sheet or tray and sprinkle with two-thirds of the oil.
4. Bake for 8–10 minutes, turning the croutons a few times during cooking so that they brown evenly.
5. Rub the chicken breasts with the remaining oil and season lightly.
6. Place on a baking sheet and roast in the oven for 10–15 minutes.
7. Bash the garlic with the flat of a knife, peel off the skin and crush with a garlic crusher.
8. Mix the garlic with the mayonnaise and thin down with the white wine vinegar.
9. Shave the cheese with a peeler.
10. Tear the lettuce into large pieces and put in a large bowl.
11. Cut the chicken into bite-size strips and scatter over the leaves, along with the croutons.
12. Add most of the dressing, season lightly and toss gently.
13. Scatter on the rest of the chicken and drizzle with the remaining dressing.
14. Arrange on a plate with the parmesan and chives and serve.

Key cookery processes and techniques
Cutting/spreading/baking/roasting/mixing/
shaving

Tips
Check if the chicken is cooked by placing the tip of
a sharp knife into the thickest part, there should
be no sign of pink flesh and the juices will run
clear.

*Alternative ways in which to enhance
the dish*
Add crispy bacon pieces to the salad, the flavour
goes well with the chicken. Classically, anchovies
are used to enhance the dish or as a garnish.

Ideas for garnishing
Save some large lettuce leaves and serve the salad
in them.

Links to the content of following courses
Hospitality Practical Cookery Int1/Hospitality
Skills for Work Int1/Home Economics Standard
Grade

 Chorizo and pasta broth

Preparation and cooking time – 50 minutes

2 portions	4 portions	Ingredients
75 g	150 g	chorizo sausage
75 g	150 g	onion
1	2	celery sticks
1	2	garlic cloves
1	2	tomatoes
2.5 ml	5 ml	olive oil
5 ml	10 ml	thyme leaves, chopped fresh
2.5 ml	5 ml	paprika
200 ml	500 ml	chicken stock
50 g	100 g	pasta shells
		seasoning

1. Cut the chorizo sausage into small, even sized pieces, the onion and celery into small dice, finely chop the garlic and dice the tomatoes.

2. Heat the olive oil in a large pan over a medium heat and cook the chorizo sausage for 3–4 minutes until crisp. Drain on kitchen paper.

3. Reduce the heat to low, add the onion and celery to the pan and season well.

4. Cook, stirring occasionally, for 6–7 minutes until softened. Add the garlic, thyme and paprika and cook, stirring, for 1–2 minutes until fragrant.

5. Add the tomatoes and cook for another minute.

6. Return the chorizo to the pan with the stock and bring to the boil, then reduce the heat and simmer, stirring occasionally, for 10 minutes.

7. Add the pasta and cook for another 10–12 minutes.

8. Strain, check the seasoning and serve.

Energy	236 kcal
Fat	10.69 g / 3.92 g saturated
Carbohydrate	25.7 g / 5.68 g sugar
Protein	10.8 g
Fibre	2.0 g

Key cookery processes and techniques
Cutting/dicing/chopping/shallow frying/simmering/boiling

Tips
Use pasta shells that are the same size as the chopped ingredients in the dish to give a uniform finish to the soup. Use cooked pasta to reduce the cooking time.

Alternative ways in which to enhance the dish
This is one of those easy soups that you can play around with: use rosemary instead of thyme or add shredded cabbage or greens at the last moment.

Ideas for garnishing
Serve with crusty bread and olive oil flavoured with freshly cut basil or use the oil produced from frying the chorizo in step 2 to drizzle over the finished soup.

Links to the content of following courses
Hospitality Practical Cookery Int1/Hospitality Skills for Work Int1/Home Economics Standard Grade

6 Cock-a-leekie soup

Preparation and cooking time – 55 minutes

2 portions	4 portions	Ingredients
1	2	chicken legs
1	1	bouquet garni
50 g	100 g	leek
25 g	50 g	onion
10 g	20 g	butter
10 g	20 g	long grain rice
2.5 ml	5 ml	parsley, chopped
		seasoning

1. Place the chicken and bouquet garni in a pot, cover with water and bring to the boil.

2. Reduce to a simmer, skim off any froth from time-to-time and cook for 30 minutes.

3. Cut the leek and onion into a small dice.

4. Melt the butter in a pan and add the leek and onion. Cook without colour for 5 minutes.

5. Remove the chicken from the stock pot, pour the stock over the leek and onion, add the bouquet garni, season and continue to cook.

6. When cool, cut the chicken into small pieces and set aside for serving.

7. Wash the rice, add to the stock and simmer for a further 20 minutes.

8. Finally, add the chicken pieces, season again, and garnish with chopped parsley just before serving.

Energy	53 kcal
Fat	0.83 g / 0.21 g saturated
Carbohydrate	6.1 g / 1.25 g sugar
Protein	5.6 g
Fibre	0.8 g

Key cookery processes and techniques
Boiling/simmering/skimming/dicing/sweating/cutting

Tips
Cut the chicken leg into two pieces to ensure correct cooking. This can be done easily by cutting through the natural joint which is roughly in the middle.

Alternative ways in which to enhance the dish
To make the classic cock-a-leekie, add some sliced prunes with the parsley prior to serving. The chicken can also be cut into julienne along with the leek.

Ideas for garnishing
Try serving this with oatcakes, freshly made if possible.

Links to the content of following courses
Hospitality Practical Cookery Int1/Hospitality Skills for Work Int1/Home Economics Standard Grade

 Samosas

Preparation and cooking time – 60 minutes

2 portions	4 portions	Ingredients
125 g	250 g	flour
30 g	60 g	butter
30 ml	60 ml	water
½	1	small onion
½	1	garlic clove
1 g	2 g	ginger root, peeled
pinch		ground turmeric
pinch		chilli powder
75 g	150 g	minced lamb
		seasoning
2 g	4 g	garam masala
10 ml	20 ml	lemon juice, fresh

Energy	511 kcal
Fat	29.93 g / 11.35 g saturated
Carbohydrate	50.1 g / 1.96 g sugar
Protein	13.6 g
Fibre	2.2 g

1. In a bowl, mix flour, half of the butter and a good pinch of salt until the mixture resembles fine breadcrumbs.

2. Pour in enough water and mix to make a smooth dough.

3. Place on a lightly floured surface and knead for 10 minutes, or until the dough is smooth and elastic.

4. Return to the bowl, cover and set aside.

5. Preheat a deep fat fryer.

6. Cut the onion into a fine dice, crush and chop the garlic and grate the ginger.

7. Melt the remaining butter in a pan, add the onion and cook for 5 minutes until they are golden brown.

8. Stir in the garlic, ginger, turmeric, chilli powder, minced lamb and seasoning.

9. Cook for about 10 minutes until the lamb is evenly brown.

10. Stir in the garam masala and lemon juice, continue cooking for 5 minutes, then remove from heat.

11. Divide the dough into 50 g balls and flatten into 15 cm circles.

12. Cut each circle in half, dampen half of the straight edge and form semicircles into cones.

13. Fill the cones with equal portions of the lamb mixture.

14. Dampen the top and bottom edges of cones, and pinch to seal.

15. Carefully lower the cones into preheated oil a few at a time and fry until golden brown, for about 2 to 3 minutes.

16. Drain on paper towels and serve warm.

Key cookery processes and techniques
Mixing/kneading/dicing/chopping/grating/stirring/rolling/filling/deep frying

Tips
When making the pastry, take care not to add too much water or it will make the dough too wet and difficult to handle. When dampening the edges of the pastry, don't use too much water as this will prevent it from sticking together.

Alternative ways in which to enhance the dish
Replace the minced lamb with minced vegetables to make a vegetarian samosa.

Ideas for garnishing
Serve with a fresh salad and a spicy tomato relish and/or a minted yoghurt dressing.

Links to the content of following courses
Hospitality Practical Cookery Int2/Hospitality Skills for Work Int2/Hospitality General Operations Int2

Chilli meat tacos

Preparation and cooking time – 45 minutes

2 portions	4 portions	Ingredients
25 g	50 g	white onion
½	1	garlic clove
2.5 ml	5 ml	oil
½	1	red chilli
½	1	green pepper
150 g	300 g	minced beef
2.5 ml	5 ml	chilli powder
100 g	200 g	tomatoes, tinned chopped
50 g	100 g	kidney beans, cooked and drained
Salsa		
1	2	tomatoes
½	1	red onion
5 ml	10 ml	lime juice
2.5 ml	5 ml	coriander, chopped
		seasoning
4	8	small tortillas

1. Chop the white onion finely and crush the garlic.

2. Heat the oil in a pan and sweat the onion and garlic.

3. Deseed and chop the chilli and pepper.

4. Add the mince to the pan and colour.

5. Add the chilli, pepper, chilli powder, tinned chopped tomatoes and kidney beans.

6. Bring to the boil, reduce to a simmer, season and cook for 20 minutes.

7. Make a salsa by chopping the tomato and red onion.

8. Mix together with the lime juice and coriander and season to taste.

9. Warm the tortillas gently in the microwave for 10–20 seconds.

10. Taste the mince for seasoning and serve in the tortillas with some of the salsa.

Key cookery processes and techniques
Chopping/crushing/sweating/simmering/mixing

Tips
When preparing the chilli, make sure that you clean the board well after use to remove any juices as they will transfer onto other foods. Be careful not to get the juices on your hands as they will leave a burning sensation for up to an hour.

Alternative ways in which to enhance the dish
The meat can be replaced by either more vegetables or fish to give a different dish.

Ideas for garnishing
Grate a little cheese and melt over the top of the tortillas to give a nice flavour and finish to the dish.

Links to the content of following courses
Hospitality Practical Cookery Int1/Hospitality Skills for Work Int1/Home Economics Standard Grade

Energy	520 kcal
Fat	10.27 g / 3.38 g saturated
Carbohydrate	83.8 g / 8.48 g sugar
Protein	28.6 g
Fibre	6.3 g

9 Chicken megankyle

Preparation and cooking time – 30 minutes

2 portions	4 portions	Ingredients
50 g	100 g	chicken, cooked
1	2	celery sticks
1	2	spring onions
2	4	cherry tomatoes
25 g	50 g	black grapes, seedless
½	1	garlic clove
2.5 ml	5 ml	tarragon, fresh, chopped
30 ml	60 ml	mayonnaise
20 ml	40 ml	natural yoghurt
		salt and freshly milled black pepper
		lettuce leaves

1. Cut the chicken into 2 cm strips, slice the celery into batons, slice the spring onion to give rounds and cut the cherry tomatoes into halves and black grapes into quarters or halves.

2. Place all in a bowl, season lightly and mix gently. Reserve in the refrigerator.

3. Crush the garlic and mix together with the tarragon, mayonnaise and yoghurt to form the dressing and season to taste.

4. Serve the salad on lettuce leaves, garnished with sprigs of watercress and accompanied by the dressing.

Energy	153 kcal
Fat	12.19 g / 1.97 g saturated
Carbohydrate	4.2 g / 3.92 g sugar
Protein	6.8 g
Fibre	0.7 g

Key cookery processes and techniques
Cutting/slicing/mixing/crushing

Tips
Don't dress the salad too early as this will make the salad leaves go limp. Black olives and feta cheese can also be used to give a fuller flavoured salad.

Alternative ways in which to enhance the dish
The mayonnaise can be replaced by a nut or olive oil to lighten the dish.

Ideas for garnishing
A crunchy toasted ciabatta crouton would be a great addition to the dish.

Links to the content of following courses
Hospitality Practical Cookery Int1/Hospitality Skills for Work Int1/Home Economics Standard Grade

10 Chicken tikka kebabs

Preparation and cooking time – 60 minutes

2 portions	4 portions	Ingredients
250 g	500 g	chicken breast
75 g	150 g	natural yoghurt, low fat
15 ml	30 ml	tikka powder
7.5 ml	15 ml	coriander, fresh, chopped
1	2	red onions
1	2	carrots
½	1	courgette
½	1	green chilli
1	2	tomatoes
		salt and freshly ground black pepper
2.5 ml	5 ml	black onion seeds
1.25 ml	2.5 ml	cumin seeds
		mint sprigs
		coriander sprigs

1. Cut the chicken into chunks.

2. Mix the yoghurt and tikka powder together in a glass or plastic bowl and add the chopped coriander.

3. Mix with the chicken, stirring well to coat.

4. Cover, chill and leave to marinate for at least 30 minutes.

5. Cut the red onion into wedges, grate the carrot and courgette, deseed and chop the chilli, and quarter, deseed and cut the tomatoes into batons.

6. Thread the chicken chunks onto skewers with the red onion wedges.

7. Make the salad by mixing together the carrots and courgettes, chilli and tomatoes.

8. Add the black onion seeds, cumin seeds, mint and coriander sprigs and season to taste.

9. Preheat the barbecue, char-grill pan or grill.

10. Cook the chicken kebabs for about 10–12 minutes, turning often, until thoroughly cooked.

11. Serve with the salad.

Key cookery processes and techniques
Cutting/mixing/chopping/stirring/marinating/grating/grilling

Tips
If using wooden skewers, remember to soak them well first to stop them burning too easily. Lightly toast the seeds in a dry frying pan to bring out their flavour. This dish could be made over two days with the chicken being marinated overnight.

Alternative ways in which to enhance the dish
Use a medium curry powder instead of the tikka powder to give a different flavour. Lamb, beef or a meaty fish would also work well instead of using chicken. You could try cutting the vegetables into julienne instead of grating them, to give a neat finish to the salad.

Ideas for garnishing
Make a dip using fresh mint, yoghurt and a little garlic to accompany this dish. Serve the kebabs in a warmed pitta bread with salad.

Links to the content of following courses
Hospitality Practical Cookery Int1/Hospitality Skills for Work Int1/Home Economics Standard Grade

Energy	214 kcal
Fat	2.7 g / 0.73 g saturated
Carbohydrate	14.5 g / 11.61 g sugar
Protein	34.2 g
Fibre	3.4 g

Smoked bacon melts

Preparation and cooking time – 40 minutes

2 portions	4 portions	Ingredients
25 g	50 g	onion
25 g	50 g	red pepper
½	1	garlic clove
50 g	100 g	smoked bacon
5 ml	10 ml	oil
50 ml	100 ml	tomato passatta
pinch		oregano
50 g	100 g	Cheddar cheese
1	2	ciabatta rolls

1. Finely dice the onion and red pepper, crush the garlic and cut the bacon into a small dice.

2. Heat the oil in a pan and add the onion, pepper, garlic and bacon. Cook gently to soften.

3. Add the passatta and reduce by half.

4. Season to taste and reserve.

5. Cut the rolls in half and toast one side.

6. Grate the cheese and reserve.

7. Divide the tomato mixture between the halved rolls and sprinkle with the oregano.

8. Top with the cheese and grill for 5 minutes or until melted.

Key cookery processes and techniques
Dicing/crushing/frying/reducing/grating/toasting/grilling

Tips
When you're toasting the roll, keep the sliced side for laying the mixture onto as it's flatter and will hold the mixture better.

Alternative ways in which to enhance the dish
Use a piece of pancetta instead of the bacon to give a different flavour or, if you want a vegetarian dish, omit the bacon. Use parmesan cheese instead of Cheddar for a stronger taste.

Ideas for garnishing
Garnish with a little crème fraîche and rocket leaves or garnish with a little cress and drizzle with chilli sauce.

Links to the content of following courses
Hospitality Practical Cookery Int1/Hospitality Skills for Work Int1/Home Economics Standard Grade

Energy	227 kcal
Fat	13.57 g / 6.33 g saturated
Carbohydrate	16.5 g / 3.45 g sugar
Protein	10.8 g
Fibre	1.3 g

12 Savoury quesadillas

Preparation and cooking time – 40 minutes

2 portions	4 portions	Ingredients
25 g	50 g	chorizo sausage
25 g	50 g	Cheddar cheese
¼	½	red pepper
¼	½	red chilli
½	1	spring onion
squeeze		lemon juice
10 ml	20 ml	natural yoghurt
		seasoning
2	4	tortillas

1. Preheat the oven to 175 °C/350 °F/gas mark 4.

2. Cut the sausage into small, even sized pieces.

3. Grate the cheese.

4. Cut the pepper and chilli into a fine dice, chop the spring onions into thin, round slices.

5. Mix the sausage, cheese, pepper, chilli, spring onion, lemon juice and yoghurt in a bowl.

6. Season to taste, divide between the tortillas and roll tightly.

7. Warm through in the oven for 5–10 minutes.

8. Cut into portions and serve.

Energy	244 kcal
Fat	7.95 g / 3.97 g saturated
Carbohydrate	35.3 g / 2.93 g sugar
Protein	10.0 g
Fibre	1.7 g

Key cookery processes and techniques
Cutting/grating/dicing/chopping/mixing

Tips
The tortillas could be heated before assembling and the quesadillas kept warm in an oven until serving.

Alternative ways in which to enhance the dish
Try making up your own ingredients using your favourite foods. You could replace the chorizo with salami or salmon.

Ideas for garnishing
The quesadillas may be accompanied by sour cream, spicy tomato salsa or a guacamole dip.

Links to the content of following courses
Hospitality Practical Cookery Int1/Hospitality Skills for Work Int1/Home Economics Standard Grade

1 Red onion and feta cheese toasts

Preparation and cooking time – 30 minutes

2 portions	4 portions	Ingredients
¼	½	baguette, cut into slices lengthways
2.5 ml	5 ml	olive oil
2.5 ml	5 ml	flat leaf parsley, chopped
15 ml	30 ml	red onion, finely diced
7.5 ml	15 ml	lemon zest
25 g	50 g	feta cheese, cut into small dice
		seasoning

1. Preheat the oven to 200 °C/400 °F/gas mark 6.

2. Scoop out excess bread to make boat shapes.

3. Place the baguette slices onto a baking tray and lightly brush with the olive oil on both sides.

4. Cook for 5–7 minutes, or until crisp and lightly golden.

5. Mix together the parsley, onion, lemon zest and feta cheese and season to taste.

6. Spoon on top of the toasts and bake in the oven for 5–10 minutes until they start to colour.

7. Serve hot.

Energy	141 kcal
Fat	4.5 g / 2.02 g saturated
Carbohydrate	21.3 g / 1.25 g sugar
Protein	5.4 g
Fibre	0.9 g

Key cookery processes and techniques
Cutting/baking/chopping/dicing/mixing

Tips
It's important that you don't saturate the bread with the oil as this will prevent it toasting (when using a pastry brush, never leave it in the liquid as you'll end up with too much of it soaking into the brush which will lead to you applying more than you need to).

Alternative ways in which to enhance the dish
You could replace the red onion with equal quantities of chopped olives and peppers to give a different flavour/colourful finish.

Ideas for garnishing
A nice sprig of the flat parsley could be used to finish off the dish. Tapenade or a pesto drizzled over the toasts would enhance the colour and flavour of the dish.

Links to the content of following courses
Hospitality Practical Cookery Int1/Hospitality Skills for Work Int1/Home Economics Standard Grade

Vegetarian starters

2 Sweetcorn cakes with avocado salsa

Preparation and cooking time – 30 minutes

2 portions	4 portions	Ingredients
125 g	250 g	sweetcorn
¼	½	red onion
½	1	egg
2	4	parsley sprigs
30 g	60 g	flour
¼ tsp	½ tsp	baking powder
		seasoning
		vegetable oil
½	1	avocado
2	4	coriander sprigs
10 ml	20 ml	lime juice
dash		tabasco

1. Place 100 g/200 g of the sweetcorn, the onion, egg, parsley, flour, baking powder and seasoning in a food processor and blitz to combine.

2. Place in a bowl and mix in the remaining sweetcorn.

3. Heat a little oil in a non-stick pan over a medium heat and place spoonfuls of the mix into the hot oil.

4. Cook for approximately one minute on each side.

5. Remove from the pan onto kitchen paper and keep warm.

6. Dice the avocado, lightly cut the coriander and mix together with the lime juice and tabasco.

7. Season to taste and serve as appropriate.

Energy	209 kcal
Fat	10.97 g / 1.94 g saturated
Carbohydrate	24.7 g / 2.8 g sugar
Protein	4.6 g
Fibre	2.9 g

Key cookery processes and techniques
Blending/mixing/shallow frying/dicing/cutting

Tips
Use an avocado that is just ripe to get the best results. If it is too ripe it will be very difficult to achieve a nice dice but it could be made into a paste instead of being chopped.

Alternative ways in which to enhance the dish
A small amount of meat or fish can be added to the cakes to give a different flavour. Try replacing half of the sweetcorn with cooked ham or salmon.

Ideas for garnishing
The avocado could be served in a small dish to accompany the sweetcorn cakes. Grill some small cherry tomatoes, 3 per portion, and serve with the cakes.

Links to the content of following courses
Hospitality Practical Cookery Int2/Hospitality Skills for Work Int2/Hospitality General Operations Int2

3 Spiced carrot and lentil soup

Preparation and cooking time – 40 minutes

2 portions	4 portions	Ingredients
1	2	garlic cloves
½	1	onion
5 g	10 g	coriander
300 g	600 g	carrots
5 g	10 g	cumin seeds
small pinch	pinch	chilli flakes
15 ml	30 ml	vegetable oil
75 g	150 g	red lentils, washed
500 ml	1 l	vegetable stock
60 ml	120 ml	milk
10 ml	20 ml	natural yoghurt

1. Chop the garlic, onion and coriander and peel and grate the carrots.

2. In a pan, carefully heat the cumin seeds and chilli flakes until they pop.

3. Remove half of the spice mixture and reserve until later.

4. Add the oil to the pan and sweat the garlic and onion without colouring.

5. Add the carrots, lentils, stock and milk and bring to the boil. Reduce the heat, season and simmer for 15–20 minutes.

6. Taste the soup and adjust the seasoning if required – the lentils should be swollen and soft.

7. Add the reserved spices and finish with the coriander and yoghurt.

Energy	234 kcal
Fat	8.99 g / 1.36 g saturated
Carbohydrate	29.5 g / 8.02 g sugar
Protein	11.3 g
Fibre	3.4 g

Key cookery processes and techniques
Chopping/peeling/grating/sweating/boiling/simmering

Tips
When 'popping' the spices, be careful not to have your pan too hot as the spices will burn very easily.

Alternative ways in which to enhance the dish
The soup could be puréed to give a smooth texture/finish. You could use ham stock and add diced ham to the dish to give a meat-based soup. Add some freshly chopped chillies, chilli powder or tabasco sauce to give the soup an additional spiced flavour.

Ideas for garnishing
The dish could also be finished with naan bread croutons – simply cut the bread into small, even sized pieces and grill them.

Links to the content of following courses
Hospitality Practical Cookery Int1/Hospitality Skills for Work Int1/Home Economics Standard Grade

Baked Brie parcel

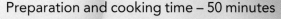

Preparation and cooking time – 50 minutes		
2 portions	**4 portions**	**Ingredients**
½	1	garlic head
5 ml	10 ml	olive oil
½	1	onion
½	1	Granny Smith apple
25 g	50 g	butter
100 g	200 g	Brie cheese
1	2	filo pastry sheets
		seasoning

1. Preheat oven to 200 °C/400 °F/gas mark 6. Place the garlic on a baking tray, and drizzle with olive oil. Roast for 15 minutes, or until soft. Set aside.

2. Slice the onions thinly and cut the apple into thicker slices.

3. Melt the butter in a frying pan over medium heat, add the onion and apple and cook carefully until tender and caramelised. Set aside.

4. Lay the filo pastry flat on the work surface and arrange the Brie on top of each sheet of pastry. Top the cheese with the apple and onion mixture. Fold the pastry over the cheese, and pinch closed to make a parcel, one per portion. Brush with melted butter.

5. Bake for about 20–25 minutes, or until golden brown. Serve warm, garnished with whole cloves of roasted garlic.

Energy	354 kcal
Fat	27.8 g / 16.01 g saturated
Carbohydrate	14.9 g / 6.96 g sugar
Protein	12.5 g
Fibre	1.8 g

Key cookery processes and techniques
Roasting/slicing/frying/baking

Tips
When working with filo pastry, make sure that you keep it covered to avoid it drying out. For more tips on working with filo pastry see Apple Strudel instructions on page 114.

Alternative ways in which to enhance the dish
After brushing the pastry with butter, you could sprinkle it with some sesame seeds to give a different finish.

Ideas for garnishing
Serve with spiced onions or pear chutney and finish with a few salad leaves.

Links to the content of following courses
Hospitality Practical Cookery Int2/Hospitality Skills for Work Int2/Hospitality General Operations Int2

5 Butternut squash soup with chilli and crème fraîche

Preparation and cooking time – 60 minutes

2 portions	4 portions	Ingredients
½	1	butternut squash
1	2	onions
1	2	garlic cloves
1	2	red chillies
15 ml	30 ml	vegetable oil
10 ml	20 ml	butter
500 ml	1 l	vegetable stock
75 ml	150 ml	crème fraîche
		seasoning

1. Heat oven to 200 °C/400 °F/gas mark 6.

2. Peel and deseed the butternut squash and cut into large cubes, about 4cm across. Cut the onion into a small dice, thinly slice the garlic and deseed and finely chop the chilli.

3. Toss the squash in a large roasting tin with half the oil. Roast for 30 minutes, turning once during cooking, until golden and soft.

4. While the squash cooks, melt the butter with the remaining oil in a large saucepan, then add the onions, garlic and three-quarters of the chilli. Cover and cook on a very low heat for 15–20 minutes until the onions are completely soft.

5. Tip the cooked squash into the pan, add the stock and the crème fraîche (save a little for garnish), then blend with a hand blender until smooth.

6. Gently reheat, then season to taste. Serve the soup in bowls with swirls of crème fraîche and a scattering of the remaining chopped chilli.

Energy	347 kcal
Fat	26.98 g / 13.64 g saturated
Carbohydrate	23.6 g / 14.4 g sugar
Protein	4.1 g
Fibre	4.1 g

Key cookery processes and techniques
Peeling/dicing/slicing/deseeding/chopping/roasting/blending

Tips
For a really silky soup, put the soup into a liquidiser and blend it in batches.

Alternative ways in which to enhance the dish
Add a few cumin seeds when roasting the vegetables. The soup can also be made in a pot where the vegetables are sweated instead of roasted.

Ideas for garnishing
Cut some squash into a small dice, cook and use as a garnish.

Links to the content of following courses
Hospitality Practical Cookery Int2/Hospitality Skills for Work Int2/Hospitality General Operations Int2

 # Roasted vegetable tart

Preparation and cooking time – 60 minutes

2 portions	4 portions	Ingredients
75 g	150 g	flour
37.5 g	75 g	margarine
pinch		salt
15–20 ml	30–40 ml	cold water
¼	½	green pepper
½	1	red onion
½	1	courgette, small
75 g	150 g	squash
25 ml	50 ml	oil
½	1	white onion
1	2	garlic cloves
10 g	20 g	butter
75 ml	150 ml	tomato passata
pinch		mixed herbs
25 ml	50 ml	pesto
		seasoning

Energy	507 kcal
Fat	34.55 g / 8.02 g saturated
Carbohydrate	43.0 g / 10.54 g sugar
Protein	8.7 g
Fibre	4.3 g

1. Preheat the oven to 200 °C/400 °F/gas mark 6.

2. Rub together the flour, salt and margarine, add just enough cold water to mix to a firm dough, wrap in cling film and put it in the fridge to chill.

3. Cut the red onion into wedges and slice the pepper, courgette and squash.

4. Put the vegetables in a roasting tin, drizzle with oil and roast in the oven for about 30 minutes.

5. Reduce the temperature of the oven to 180 °C/360 °F/gas mark 4.

6. Roll the pastry and cut into individual circles.

7. Prick the pastry all over with a fork, put a layer of greaseproof paper over it, cover with a baking sheet and bake for about 20 minutes.

8. Finely chop the white onion and garlic and fry in oil for a few minutes until softened.

9. Add the passatta, herbs and seasoning and simmer, uncovered, for about 10 minutes until the sauce has reduced and is quite thick.

10. When the pastry case is ready, remove the baking sheet and greaseproof paper, spread the tomato sauce over the base of the tart and top with the roasted vegetables.

11. Drizzle with the pesto and serve.

Key cookery processes and techniques
Rubbing in/chilling/cutting/slicing/roasting/
baking/frying/reducing

Tips
Try not to assemble the tart too early as the pastry
will go soggy.

*Alternative ways in which to enhance the
dish*
Try mixing some ripened mozzarella through the
cooked vegetables.

Ideas for garnishing
Accompany with a salad of rocket leaves and shaved
parmesan cheese.

Links to the content of following courses
Hospitality Practical Cookery Int2/Hospitality
Skills for Work Int2/Hospitality General Operations
Int2

Spinach and potato gnocchi

Preparation and cooking time – 60 minutes

2 portions	4 portions	Ingredients
200 g	400 g	floury potatoes, peeled
50 g	100 g	spinach
50 g	100 g	Cheddar cheese, grated
1	2	egg yolks, free-range
		salt and freshly ground black pepper
100 g	200 g	plain flour
		semolina or rice flour, to coat
		olive oil
20 ml	45 ml	butter

Energy	488 kcal
Fat	21.81 g / 12.19 g saturated
Carbohydrate	60.6 g / 1.82 g sugar
Protein	15.7 g
Fibre	3.5 g

1. For the gnocchi, chop the potatoes into even-sized pieces, then steam until tender.

2. Mash the potatoes or pass them through a sieve.

3. Cook the spinach in a little boiling water for 30 seconds, then cool under cold running water.

4. Squeeze out all the water, chop the spinach very finely, then stir into the potato mash.

5. Add three-quarters of the cheese, egg yolk(s) and butter and season well with salt and freshly ground black pepper.

6. Add most of the plain flour and quickly work it into the potato.

7. Cut the dough into three or four pieces and roll each into a long tubular shape about the thickness of your finger.

8. Cut off pieces 2.5 cm long and roll each one into an oblong.

9. As you go, keep the gnocchi on a tray, sprinkled with semolina or rice flour.

10. To cook the gnocchi, drop carefully into a large saucepan of simmering water, taking care not to overcrowd the pan or the gnocchi will stick.

11. The gnocchi are done when they float to the top.

12. Remove the cooked gnocchi with a slotted spoon onto a tray and sprinkle with the remaining cheese.

13. Place under a hot grill for a minute to melt the cheese and serve hot.

Key cookery processes and techniques
Peeling/chopping/steaming/mashing/grating/
shaping/simmering/grilling

Tips
If the dough feels as if it is not too sticky to roll
out, tear off a small piece, roll it into a ball and
drop it into boiling water to test. If it floats to the
top and holds its shape firmly do not add any more
flour to the dough. If it breaks apart add a little
more flour and test again.

Alternative ways in which to enhance the dish
Serve with a sauce made from 30 ml chopped fresh
sage leaves, 2 garlic cloves, finely chopped, and
2 tbs chopped walnut halves.

Ideas for garnishing
A lightly dressed bowl of salad leaves goes well
with this dish as does some lightly wilted spinach
and parmesan shavings.

Links to the content of following courses
Hospitality Practical Cookery Int2/Hospitality
Skills for Work Int2/Hospitality General Operations
Int2

Potato and celery pancake with sweet chilli

Preparation and cooking time – 45 minutes

2 portions	4 portions	Ingredients
1	2	celery sticks
1	2	floury potatoes, large
5 ml	10 ml	coriander
		sweet chilli sauce
pinch		chilli powder
		olive oil for frying
		seasoning

1. Preheat the oven to 220 °C/425 °F/gas mark 7.

2. Cut the celery into fine strips, peel and grate the potato and chop the coriander.

3. Mix the celery, grated potato and coriander together. Season, add a few drops of chilli sauce and the chilli powder.

4. Divide the mixture into equal portions and shape into round pancakes.

5. Fry for 5–6 minutes in the oil in a shallow pan turning over once they have set to lightly brown.

6. Transfer the pancakes to a lightly oiled baking tray and place in the oven for 15 minutes to finish off the cooking.

7. Place the pancakes on plates and drizzle with the chilli sauce to serve.

Key cookery processes and techniques
Cutting/peeling/grating/chopping/mixing/shaping/stir frying/baking

Tips
Make sure to fry both sides of the potato cake evenly so that it remains crisp. If you can't get a floury potato, e.g. Maris Piper, add a little beaten egg to help bind the mixture and remember not to wash the potatoes after grating them, simply squeeze excess moisture out.

Alternative ways in which to enhance the dish
Serve with a green salad or roasted vegetables.

Ideas for garnishing
Garnish with roasted vegetables or vegetable crisps.

Links to the content of following courses
Hospitality Practical Cookery Int2/Hospitality Skills for Work Int2/Hospitality General Operations Int2

Energy	238 kcal
Fat	13.08 g / 6.09 g saturated
Carbohydrate	22.3 g / 1.54 g sugar
Protein	9.2 g
Fibre	2.0 g

CHAPTER 3
Main courses

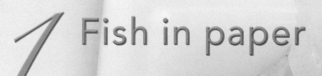

1 Fish in paper

Preparation and cooking time – 30 minutes

2 portions	4 portions	Ingredients
50 g	100 g	leek
50 g	100 g	carrot
½	1	onion
10 g	20 g	fennel bulb
1	2	garlic cloves
½	1	bay leaf
10	20	coriander seeds
2	4	fish fillets
20 g	40 g	butter
		seasoning

1. Preheat the oven to 180 °C/360 °F/gas mark 4.

2. Cut the leek, carrot, onion and fennel into julienne and chop the garlic.

3. Take a sheet of baking parchment and lightly butter one side.

4. Place the julienned vegetables and the garlic in the middle of the baking parchment.

5. Place a piece of bay leaf and coriander seeds on top of the vegetables.

6. Fold the fillet of fish in half, place on top of the vegetables and season well.

7. Place a few knobs of butter on the fish and fold the baking parchment to seal it.

8. Place on a baking tray and bake for 10–12 minutes or until the fish is cooked.

Energy	229 kcal
Fat	9.8 g / 5.42 g saturated
Carbohydrate	6.5 g / 5.01 g sugar
Protein	29.6 g
Fibre	2.3 g

Key cookery processes and techniques
Cutting/chopping/baking

Tips
Ensure there are no spaces in the baking parchment or the steam will escape; greased silver foil can be used instead as it is easier to handle. If the fish is overcooked there will be no traces of oils in the flesh, and will it will be firm and dry to touch. This method of cookery is healthy because of the low fat content and is an excellent way of cooking fish, vegetables and chicken.

Alternative ways in which to enhance the dish
Shellfish can be added to give a different flavour and finish to this dish.

Ideas for garnishing
Serve with steamed vegetables and potatoes to give a healthy dish.

Links to the content of following courses
Hospitality Practical Cookery Int2/Hospitality Skills for Work Int2/Hospitality General Operations Int2

Garlic chilli salmon with citrus risotto

Preparation and cooking time – 40 minutes

2 portions	4 portions	Ingredients
¼	½	onion
½	1	lemon
½	1	red chilli
½	1	garlic clove
10 g	20 g	coriander
300 g	600 g	salmon
7.5 ml	15 ml	vegetable oil
15 ml	30 ml	olive oil
15 g	30 g	butter
100 g	200 g	short grain rice (Arborio or alternative)
500 ml	1 l	chicken stock
		seasoning

1. Cut the onion into a small dice, zest and juice the lemon, finely chop the chilli, garlic and coriander.

2. Cut the salmon into even sized pieces and reserve in the refrigerator.

3. In a pan, add the oil, onion and half the butter. Cook until the onion is soft but not coloured.

4. Add the rice and cook for 1–2 minutes; gradually add the stock a little at a time – this should take approx. 15 minutes (the rice should be soft).

5. Remove pan from heat and stir in remaining butter, lemon zest, lemon juice and seasoning.

6. Cover the pan and leave for 3 minutes for flavours to develop.

7. Heat the olive oil in a frying pan and add the salmon. Cook for 1 min, add the chilli and garlic then cook for another minute.

8. Remove from the heat, mix in the coriander and season lightly.

9. Spoon the risotto into bowls, top with the salmon and drizzle the pan juices over the food.

Key cookery processes and techniques
Cutting/zesting/juicing/chopping/shallow frying

Tips
Make sure that when adding the stock gradually it is absorbed before you add some more. This will help to create the correct texture for the rice.

Alternative ways in which to enhance the dish
Other types of fish/shellfish can be used for this dish, e.g. cod, haddock or prawns.

Ideas for garnishing
A crisp salad dressed with lemon oil and crusty bread.

Links to the content of following courses
Hospitality Practical Cookery Int2/Hospitality Skills for Work Int2/Hospitality General Operations Int2

Energy	552 kcal
Fat	29.97 g / 7.2 g saturated
Carbohydrate	46.0 g / 2.06 g sugar
Protein	34.0 g
Fibre	0.6 g

3 Fish linguini in garlic butter

Preparation and cooking time – 50 minutes

2 portions	4 portions	Ingredients
100 g	200 g	linguini pasta
100 g	200 g	mussels
25 ml	50 ml	fish stock
5 g	10 g	parsley
1	2	garlic cloves
50 g	100 g	butter
2.5 ml	5 ml	lemon juice
100 g	200 g	cod fillet
50 g	100 g	peeled prawns
		seasoning

1. Cook the pasta in boiling salted water for 12–15 minutes until tender, drain and refresh.

2. Put the mussels into a large pan with the fish stock, cover and cook over a high heat for 3–4 minutes or until opened.

3. Tip into a colander set over a bowl so you can collect the juices.

4. Remove the meat from most of the shells; leave a few intact.

5. Place the cooking liquor into a pan and reduce until there are 2 tablespoons left.

6. Chop the parsley. Preheat the oven to 200°C/400°F/gas mark 6.

7. For the garlic butter: crush the garlic with a little salt, mix in a bowl with the butter, lemon juice, parsley and freshly ground pepper.

8. Cut the cod into 2cm dice, heat a non-stick pan and sear, then place on a tray, brush with the garlic butter and bake for 2–3 minutes.

9. Melt the remaining garlic butter, add the reduced cooking liquor, prawns and cooked mussels.

10. Mix in the cooked pasta and heat gently. Carefully mix in the cod.

11. Place the mixture onto warmed plates, spoon over the cooking juices and serve.

Key cookery processes and techniques
Boiling/reducing/chopping/searing/baking/mixing

Tips
If there are any mussels open prior to you cooking them, discard them as they are unsafe to eat.

Alternative ways in which to enhance the dish
The fish could be replaced with chicken and chorizo sausage to give a different flavour. Plan ahead and make fresh pasta.

Ideas for garnishing
The dish could be finished with some freshly grated parmesan cheese and chopped flat parsley.

Links to the content of following courses
Hospitality Practical Cookery Int2/Hospitality Skills for Work Int2/Hospitality General Operations Int2

Energy	457 kcal
Fat	22.87 g / 13.45 g saturated
Carbohydrate	39.4 g / 1.33 g sugar
Protein	26.0 g
Fibre	1.6 g

4 Honey flavoured haddock with a warm potato salad

Preparation and cooking time – 60 minutes

2 portions	4 portions	Ingredients
1	2	oranges
2 cm	4 cm	ginger root, peeled
½	1	garlic clove
10 ml	20 ml	sesame oil
20 ml	40 ml	soy sauce
20 ml	40 ml	honey
2	4	haddock fillets
100 g	200 g	new potatoes
1	2	limes
1	2	red chillies
2	4	spring onions
¼	½	green pepper
50 ml	100 ml	olive oil
pinch		cayenne pepper
25 g	50 g	rocket leaves
		seasoning

1. Zest and juice the oranges, grate the ginger and chop the garlic. Whisk together with the sesame oil, soy sauce and honey.

2. Pour over the haddock and marinate for 30 minutes.

3. Scrape the potatoes and slice 1 cm thick. Cook in boiling, salted water until just tender.

4. Zest and juice the lime, chop the chilli and finely dice the spring onions and green pepper.

5. Mix together the lime zest and juice, chilli and olive oil, season to taste.

6. Once the potatoes are cooked, drain and immediately toss in the lime vinaigrette. Allow to cool slightly before adding the finely diced spring onion, green pepper and cayenne pepper.

7. Remove the haddock from the marinade and cook under the grill for about 2 minutes on each side.

8. Arrange the potato salad on a plate with the rocket leaves. Place the cooked haddock on top of the potatoes.

Key cookery processes and techniques
Zesting/juicing/grating/chopping/whisking/marinating/boiling/dicing/grilling

Tips
Make sure you wash your hands after touching the chilli as the juices that remain will be very hot/create a burning sensation on your skin.

Alternative ways in which to enhance the dish
Iceberg lettuce may be used instead of the more peppery rocket leaves.

Ideas for garnishing
Garnish with lightly cooked green beans.

Links to the content of following courses
Hospitality Practical Cookery Int2/Hospitality Skills for Work Int2/Hospitality General Operations Int2

Energy	325 kcal
Fat	6.65 g / 1 g saturated
Carbohydrate	31.4 g / 22.54 g sugar
Protein	37.2 g
Fibre	3.3 g

5 Prawn nasi goreng

Preparation and cooking time – 30 minutes

2 portions	4 portions	Ingredients
1	2	eggs
22.5 ml	45 ml	vegetable oil
3	6	spring onions
½	1	carrot
150 g	300 g	white cabbage
½	1	garlic clove
150 g	300 g	long grain rice, cooked
100 g	200 g	prawns, small, cooked and peeled
15 ml	30 ml	soy sauce, dark
7.5 ml	15 ml	tomato ketchup
10 g	20 g	brown sugar
10 ml	20 ml	sesame oil
10 ml	20 ml	chilli sauce
few		chives
		seasoning

1. Beat the egg(s).

2. Heat 15 ml oil in a large frying pan over a medium heat ensuring it coats the pan.

3. Add the egg and swirl the mixture so that it spreads thinly over the surface of the pan. Let it set for about 30 seconds, then loosen the edges with a fish slice and flip it over. Cook for 10 seconds, then remove to a chopping board, roll up and slice into ribbons. Set aside.

4. Slice the spring onions, finely dice the carrot, finely slice the cabbage, crush the garlic and chop the chives.

5. Heat the remaining oil in the same pan and add the spring onions, carrot and cabbage and stir fry for 3 minutes until tender. Add the garlic, rice and prawns and toss with the vegetables.

6. Combine the soy sauce, ketchup, sugar, sesame oil and chilli sauce. Stir through the rice mixture and season to taste.

7. Serve topped with the egg and chives.

Key cookery processes and techniques
Beating/slicing/dicing/stir frying

Tips
A curry paste is traditionally made using shrimp and tomato paste, but this no-fuss version with ketchup tastes surprisingly authentic.

Alternative ways in which to enhance the dish
Instead of prawns, you could use a firm-fleshed white fish such as pollack. Alternatively, you can serve this dish with a fried egg on top if you prefer.

Ideas for garnishing
Prawn crackers would be a great accompaniment for this dish when garnishing.

Links to the content of following courses
Hospitality Practical Cookery Int2/Hospitality Skills for Work Int2/Hospitality General Operations Int2

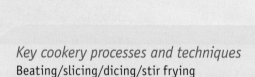

Energy	564 kcal
Fat	20.95 g / 3.09 g saturated
Carbohydrate	78.2 g / 12.05 g sugar
Protein	20.6 g
Fibre	3.0 g

6 Hoisin salmon burritos

Preparation and cooking time – 40 minutes

2 portions	4 portions	Ingredients
½	1	lime
20 g	40 g	coriander
50 ml	100 ml	hoisin sauce
10 ml	20 ml	olive oil
dash	dash	tabasco sauce
100 g	200 g	salmon
75 ml	150 ml	sweet chilli jam
25 g	50 g	spring onion
25 g	50 g	red onion
4	8	tortillas
		oil for frying
		seasoning

1. Juice the lime and chop the coriander.

2. Whisk the lime juice, hoisin sauce, olive oil, tabasco sauce and coriander in a bowl until combined.

3. Cut the salmon into thin strips.

4. Pour the liquid over the salmon and coat thoroughly. Leave to marinate for as long as possible.

5. Cut the spring onion into thin rounds and finely chop the red onion.

6. Wrap the tortillas in tin foil and warm gently in the oven.

7. Heat a non-stick frying pan and add a little oil.

8. Fry the spring onion and red onion until soft, taking care not too colour them too much.

9. Add the salmon and fry for approximately 1 minute on each side until nicely cooked.

10. Place in the tortillas and roll up, cut in half then serve with the sweet chilli jam and accompaniments as desired.

Key cookery processes and techniques
Juicing/chopping/whisking/cutting/marinating/ stir frying

Tips
Take care when reheating the wraps as they will dry out very quickly and you will find it very difficult to fold them. You can also heat them for 10–20 seconds in the microwave.

Alternative ways in which to enhance the dish
Serve with a red pepper and coriander low fat mayonnaise.

Ideas for garnishing
Spring onion, shredded lettuce leaves and red pepper could be rolled up with the salmon.

Links to the content of following courses
Hospitality Practical Cookery Int1/Hospitality Skills for Work Int1/Home Economics Standard Grade

Energy	718 kcal
Fat	42.61 g / 6.25 g saturated
Carbohydrate	69.1 g / 3.89 g sugar
Protein	18.8 g
Fibre	2.7 g

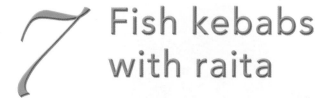

Fish kebabs with raita

Preparation and cooking time – 60 minutes

2 portions	4 portions	Ingredients
Kebabs		
75 g	150 g	cod fillet
75 g	150 g	salmon fillet
¼	½	lime
25 g	50 g	fennel
1	2	green chillies
10 g	20 g	coriander
1	2	garlic cloves
1	2	spring onions
1 cm	2 cm	ginger root, peeled
10 g	20 g	ground fennel seeds
10 g	20 g	ground coriander seeds
		oil for brushing
Raita		
¼	½	cucumber
10 g	20 g	dill
¼	½	garlic clove
2 g	4 g	mustard seeds
1 g	2 g	cumin seeds
1	2	curry leaves
125 ml	250 ml	natural yoghurt
		seasoning

Energy	216 kcal
Fat	13.84 g / 2.11 g saturated
Carbohydrate	6.8 g / 5.98 g sugar
Protein	19.8 g
Fibre	1.0 g

1. Preheat the oven to 180 °C/360 °F/gas mark 4; if you are using the grill turn it on 5 minutes prior to using it.

2. In a food processor blend half the cod to a smooth paste.

3. Cut the remaining cod and salmon into small dice.

4. Zest and juice the lime, finely dice the fennel and chilli, chop the coriander and garlic, slice the spring onions and grate the ginger.

5. Combine the cod paste with the remaining cod, salmon and lime zest.

6. Add the remaining ingredients for the kebabs and mix well.

7. Mould the mixture onto skewers or shape into fish cakes.

8. Place the fish onto a non-stick tray and then lightly brush with some oil.

9. Grill or bake for 3 minutes before turning. Cook for a further 2–3 minutes or until firm to touch.

10. For the raita, grate the cucumber, chop the dill and crush the garlic.

11. Heat a small pan and light fry the seeds and curry leaves until fragrant. Allow to cool.

12. Squeeze out any excess water from the cucumber and mix with the yoghurt.

13. Mix in the dill, garlic, seeds and season to taste.

14. Serve as appropriate.

Key cookery processes and techniques
Blending/dicing/zesting/juicing/chopping/
slicing/grating/mixing/grilling/baking/crushing

Tips
Wet your hands with water to stop the mixture
from sticking to your fingers when moulding.
The dish can be grilled, shallow fried or baked
depending on which cookery process requires to be
covered. Although time consuming, 25 g of fennel
could be cut into brunoise. The fish can be blended
into a paste the day before if required.

Alternative ways in which to enhance the dish
Any fish can be used, even a mixture of half fish
and half prawns if you like. A green Thai curry paste
could be used instead of the spices; this will cut
down on the preparation time.

Ideas for garnishing
You can use lemon grass instead of wooden skewers
to give a different flavour and finish, and serve
with noodles.

Links to the content of following courses
Hospitality Practical Cookery Int2/Hospitality
Skills for Work Int2/Hospitality General
Operations Int2

Turkish meatballs in tomato sauce

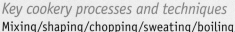

Preparation and cooking time – 45 minutes

2 portions	4 portions	Ingredients
5 g	10 g	ground cumin
5 g	10 g	allspice powder
100 g	200 g	lamb, minced
50 g	100 g	beef, minced
15 g	30 g	breadcrumbs
½	1	egg
50 g	100 g	onion
1	2	garlic cloves
15 ml	30 ml	vegetable oil
50 ml	100 ml	tomato passatta
50 g	100 g	tomatoes, tinned chopped
100 ml	200 ml	vegetable stock seasoning

1. Mix together the cumin, allspice, minced lamb and beef, breadcrumbs and egg, and season. Shape into balls and reserve in the fridge.

2. Finely chop the onion and crush the garlic.

3. Heat half the oil in a pan, add the onion and garlic and sweat for 5 minutes.

4. Add the passatta, tomatoes and stock.

5. Bring to the boil, season to taste and reduce to a simmer.

6. Heat the remaining oil in a pan and brown the meatballs carefully.

7. Remove the meatballs onto kitchen paper then place carefully into the tomato sauce.

8. Cook out for 10 minutes in the gently simmering liquid.

9. Taste again for seasoning prior to serving.

Key cookery processes and techniques
Mixing/shaping/chopping/sweating/boiling/ simmering/shallow frying

Tips
When shaping the balls, moisten your hands lightly to avoid the mixture sticking.

Alternative ways in which to enhance the dish
The dish could be served with boiled, steamed or braised rice.

Ideas for garnishing
Warm pitta bread or poppadom crisps could be used as a garnish. The dish could be finished with some freshly chopped mint leaves.

Links to the content of following courses
Hospitality Practical Cookery Int2/Hospitality Skills for Work Int2/Hospitality General Operations Int2

Energy	272 kcal
Fat	17.71 g / 5.05 g saturated
Carbohydrate	10.4 g / 3.59 g sugar
Protein	19.3 g
Fibre	1.1 g

Spicy lamb kofta with hot and cold dressings

Preparation and cooking time – 50 minutes

2 portions	4 portions	Ingredients
½	1	onion
½	1	garlic clove
¼	½	red chilli
50 g	100 g	cucumber
200 g	400 g	lamb, minced
1	2	ground cumin, pinch
1	2	ground cinnamon, pinch
½	1	egg
2	4	skewers
75 g	150 g	tomatoes, ripe
5 ml	10 ml	parsley, chopped
75 g	150 g	Greek yoghurt
5 ml	10 ml	oil
2	4	pitta breads
		seasoning

1. Finely chop the onion, crush the garlic, chop the chilli and grate the cucumber.

2. In a bowl, mix together the lamb, onion, spices and egg. Season and divide into 8/16 pieces.

3. Shape into balls and thread onto skewers, leaving a gap of 1 cm between each.

4. Blanch the tomatoes, skin and deseed.

5. Cut into small dice and mix together with the red chilli and parsley. Season to taste and reserve until use.

6. Mix together the yoghurt, cucumber and garlic – reserve until use.

7. Heat the grill, oil a tray and place the koftas on it.

8. Grill for approx 10 minutes, turning to ensure an even cooking.

9. Open the pitta breads, warm and serve the koftas in them along with the hot and cold dressings.

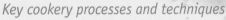

Key cookery processes and techniques
Chopping/crushing/grating/blanching/skinning/deseeding/mixing/grilling

Tips
Dampen your hands with a little water prior to shaping the koftas; this will prevent them sticking to you. If you use wooden skewers, soak them in water for 30 minutes first – this will prevent them from burning whilst the meat is cooking. An extra precaution is to protect the ends with silver foil.

Alternative ways in which to enhance the dish
The dish could be served with boiled rice which has been flavoured with pine nuts.

Ideas for garnishing
A simple salad of lettuce, tomato and cucumber goes well with this dish. Try cutting the pitta bread in half and stuffing one piece with some salad and the other with the koftas.

Links to the content of following courses
Hospitality Practical Cookery Int2/Hospitality Skills for Work Int2/Hospitality General Operations Int2

Energy	452 kcal
Fat	20.24 g / 8.66 g saturated
Carbohydrate	39.7 g / 7.36 g sugar
Protein	30.3 g
Fibre	2.6 g

 Chicken burgers
with sweetcorn
relish

Preparation and cooking time – 50 minutes

2 portions	4 portions	Ingredients
¼	½	onion
½	1	garlic clove
¼	½	red pepper
5 ml	10 ml	parsley
5 ml	10 ml	chives
10 ml	25 ml	sunflower oil
150 g	300 g	chicken, minced
25 ml	50 ml	Greek yoghurt
15 g	30 g	breadcrumbs, fresh
25 g	50 g	Cheddar cheese
¼	½	red chilli
1 tsp	2 tsp	brown sugar
15 ml	30 ml	malt vinegar
75 g	150 g	sweetcorn nibs
5 ml	10 ml	coriander, chopped
		seasoning
2	4	sesame seed buns

Energy	402 kcal
Fat	15.64 g / 5.17 g saturated
Carbohydrate	40.3 g / 7.94 g sugar
Protein	27.5 g
Fibre	2.4 g

1. Finely chop the onion, garlic, red pepper, parsley and chives.

2. Heat the oil in a pan and sweat the onion and garlic until soft.

3. Add the red pepper to the pan and cook for a further 2–3 minutes.

4. Remove into a mixing bowl, allow to cool, add in the chicken, yoghurt, breadcrumbs, parsley, chives and cheese. Mix well and season.

5. Divide the mixture into 2 or 4 and shape into burgers with a palette knife; reserve in the refrigerator until use.

6. Finely chop the red chilli.

7. Heat the vinegar and sugar in a pan and dissolve the sugar.

8. Add the chilli and sweetcorn and cook for 2–3 minutes, allowing the mixture to reduce slightly.

9. Preheat the grill.

10. Remove the relish pan from the heat, add the coriander and season to taste.

11. Cook the burgers under the grill for approx. 8–10 minutes, turning to ensure even cooking.

12. Warm the buns, cut them open, place the burger inside and finish with the relish.

Key cookery processes and techniques
Chopping/sweating/mixing/shaping/chilling/reducing/grilling

Tips
When shaping the burgers, lightly flour the work surface as this will prevent the mixture sticking. When cooking the burgers, keep them moist by brushing lightly with oil – this will ensure that they do not dry out.

Alternative ways in which to enhance the dish
You could replace the chicken with minced beef or fish. Depending on availability, you could remove/add different herbs – tarragon goes very well with chicken.

Ideas for garnishing
A fresh salad and lemon mayonnaise would go well with this dish. As an accompaniment, you could try serving spiced potato wedges.

Links to the content of following courses
Hospitality Practical Cookery Int2/Hospitality Skills for Work Int2/Hospitality General Operations Int2

Chicken with mushroom and tarragon

Preparation and cooking time – 50 minutes

2 portions	4 portions	Ingredients
1	2	shallots
1	2	garlic cloves
5 g	10 g	parsley
5 g	10 g	tarragon
6	12	mushrooms
1	2	tomatoes
4	8	chicken leg meat, boned
10 g	20 g	flour
20 ml	40 ml	vegetable oil
200 ml	400 ml	gravy
		seasoning

1. Preheat the oven to 180 °C/360 °F/gas mark 4.

2. Finely chop the shallots, crush the garlic, chop the parsley and tarragon, and wipe and slice the mushrooms.

3. Blanch the tomatoes in boiling water for 10 seconds and plunge into ice-cold water.

4. Remove the skin, cut into quarters, deseed and then dice the flesh.

5. Season the flour and coat the chicken pieces with it.

6. Heat the oil in a large pan and carefully add the chicken pieces.

7. When brown, remove onto a tray and place in the oven for 10–12 minutes.

8. Add the shallots and garlic to the pan and cook until soft for about 3–5 minutes.

9. Add the mushrooms and cook for a further 5 minutes over a low heat.

10. Add the gravy and bring to the boil.

11. Remove the chicken from the oven and place in the sauce.

12. Add the tomatoes, parsley and tarragon and cook over a low heat to mix the flavours for 5 minutes.

13. Taste for seasoning and serve.

Key cookery processes and techniques
Chopping/crushing/slicing/blanching/peeling/deseeding/dicing/shallow frying

Tips
When preparing the tomatoes for blanching, remove the 'eye' from the tomato. This will help the water penetrate and loosen the skin, making it easier to remove.

Alternative ways in which to enhance the dish
The dish could be made with chicken breast meat instead of leg meat. The breast meat would only take 8–10 minutes to cook in the oven.

Ideas for garnishing
Boiled or braised potatoes could be served as an accompaniment for this dish.

Links to the content of following courses
Hospitality Practical Cookery Int2/Hospitality Skills for Work Int2/Hospitality General Operations Int2

Energy	265 kcal
Fat	15.38 g /1.97 g saturated
Carbohydrate	11.2 g / 3.31 g sugar
Protein	21.1 g
Fibre	1.5 g

5 Chicken fajitas

Preparation and cooking time – 30 minutes

2 portions	4 portions	Ingredients
200 g	400 g	chicken breast
1	2	red onions, small
½	1	green pepper
½	1	red pepper
5 ml	10 ml	coriander
30 ml	60 ml	vegetable oil
5 ml	10 ml	fajita spice mix
200 g	400 g	tomatoes, tinned chopped
2	4	tortillas, floured
		seasoning

1. Cut the chicken into strips the length of your little finger.

2. Cut the onion into slices, the peppers into the same size as the chicken and chop the coriander.

3. Heat the oil in a pan and when hot add the chicken pieces.

4. When browned, drain and place in a bowl and mix through the fajita spice.

6. Add the onion and pepper to the pan and fry for 2–3 minutes.

7. Add the tomatoes, coriander and chicken, bring to the boil and simmer for 3–5 minutes.

8. Warm the tortillas, fill with some chicken and serve.

Energy	440 kcal
Fat	17.23 g / 2.13 g saturated
Carbohydrate	43.7 g / 9.61 g sugar
Protein	30.4 g
Fibre	4.2 g

Key cookery processes and techniques
Cutting/slicing/chopping/shallow frying/simmering

Tips
To warm the tortillas, place in a microwave for 10–20 seconds. Or, if you would like to give them some colour, warm carefully in a dry frying pan.

Alternative ways in which to enhance the dish
You could use spring onions instead of red onions for a different taste/colour.

Ideas for garnishing
Try a selection of dips to go with your tortillas such as guacamole, sour cream or garlic mayonnaise. For the more adventurous, when serving to your guests, allow them the opportunity to roll the tortillas themselves.

Links to the content of following courses
Hospitality Practical Cookery Int1/Hospitality Skills for Work Int1/Home Economics Standard Grade

6 Chicken and rice

Preparation and cooking time – 45 minutes

2 portions	4 portions	Ingredients
1	2	onions, small
1	2	garlic cloves
4	8	mushrooms
15 ml	30 ml	vegetable oil
200 g	400 g	chicken leg meat
10 ml	20 ml	curry paste
100 g	200 g	long grain rice
200 ml	400 ml	chicken stock
25 g	50 g	peas, cooked
		seasoning

1. Chop the onion and garlic and quarter the mushrooms.

2. Add the oil to a pan, brown the chicken meat then remove onto kitchen paper.

3. Add the onion and garlic to the pan and sweat for 2–3 minutes until soft.

4. Add the mushrooms and cook over a low heat for a further 3 minutes.

5. Add the curry paste and cook out for 2–3 minutes.

6. Add the chicken, rice and stock to the pan and bring to the boil.

7. Reduce to a simmer, cover with a tight fitting lid and cook gently for 15 minutes.

8. Add peas, adjust the seasoning and serve.

Energy	412 kcal
Fat	13.24 g /1.72 g saturated
Carbohydrate	49.7 g /3.63 g sugar
Protein	26.4 g
Fibre	1.9 g

Key cookery processes and techniques
Chopping/shallow frying/sweating/simmering

Tips
Wash the rice before use to remove impurities/ extra starch. This will help to give the dish a nicer flavour. The dish can be finished in the oven rather than on top of the stove – place the pot in an oven at 175 °C/350 °F/gas mark 4 for 15 minutes or until the stock has been absorbed.

Alternative ways in which to enhance the dish
When cooked, 25 g of unsalted butter can be forked through the dish to give a richer taste. The chicken/ chicken stock can be replaced by more vegetables/ vegetable stock to give a vegetarian alternative.

Ideas for garnishing
Some freshly chopped coriander works well with this dish, along with naan bread and curry sauce.

Links to the content of following courses
Hospitality Practical Cookery Int2/Hospitality Skills for Work Int2/Hospitality General Operations Int2

7 Pork satay sticks

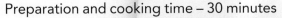

Preparation and cooking time – 30 minutes

2 portions	4 portions	Ingredients
½	1	onion
½	1	garlic clove
250 g	500 g	pork, minced
½	1	egg
7.5 ml	15 ml	soy sauce
25 g	50 g	breadcrumbs
7.5 ml	15 ml	vegetable oil
10 ml	20 ml	ginger root, grated
7.5 ml	15 ml	curry powder
175 ml	350 ml	evaporated milk
5 ml	10 ml	cornflour
15 ml	30 ml	peanut butter

1. Cut the onion into a small dice and crush the garlic.

2. Combine the mince with the egg, soy sauce and breadcrumbs and mix well.

3. Shape into balls to give six per portion, cover and reserve in the refrigerator until use.

4. Heat the oil and cook the meatballs, turning to ensure an even cooking.

5. Thread onto skewers and set aside, keeping warm.

6. Add the onion, garlic and ginger to the pan and cook for 2 minutes to soften them.

7. Stir in the curry powder and mix well.

8. Mix a little evaporated milk with the cornflour to make a paste.

9. Add the remaining milk, cornflour paste and peanut butter to the pan.

10. Bring to the boil and simmer for 1 minute.

11. Serve with the sticks.

Key cookery processes and techniques
Dicing/crushing/mixing/grating/shaping/shallow frying/simmering

Tips
Make sure that the meatballs are all the same size so that they take the same time to cook.

Alternative ways in which to enhance the dish
The sauce could be blended to give a smooth consistency.

Ideas for garnishing
Fresh coriander to garnish the finished dish, along with some prawn crackers.

Links to the content of following courses
Hospitality Practical Cookery Int1/Hospitality Skills for Work Int1/Home Economics Standard Grade

Energy	571 kcal
Fat	21.7 g / 8.19 g saturated
Carbohydrate	58.5 g / 44.56 g sugar
Protein	39.0 g
Fibre	1.5 g

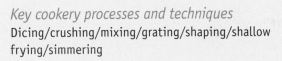

Beef patties with tomato spaghetti

Preparation and cooking time – 45 minutes

2 portions	4 portions	Ingredients
½	1	garlic clove
10 ml	20 ml	parsley
250 g	500 g	beef, minced
75 g	150 g	breadcrumbs
½	1	egg, large
pinch		cumin powder
50 ml	100 ml	vegetable oil
35 ml	75 ml	water
5 g	10 g	sugar
250 g	500 g	tomato passatta
100 g	200 g	spaghetti
		seasoning

Energy	847 kcal
Fat	45.59 g /9.5 g saturated
Carbohydrate	72.7 g /8.83 g sugar
Protein	41.3 g
Fibre	3.3 g

1. Finely chop the garlic and parsley.

2. Mix well with the mince, breadcrumbs, egg and cumin, and season. Refrigerate for 10 minutes.

3. Divide the mixture into even sized pieces and shape with a palette knife into small sausage-shaped barrels.

4. Heat the oil in a frying pan and fry the patties for 2–3 minutes each side until brown.

5. Remove the patties onto kitchen paper and carefully pour off the excess oil from the pan.

6. Add the water and sugar to the pan and dissolve the sugar.

7. Add the passatta, season, bring to the boil and simmer for 5 minutes.

8. Carefully place the patties into the pan, cover with a tight fitting lid and cook out for 20 minutes.

9. Bring a pot of water to the boil for the spaghetti.

10. Lightly season, add the spaghetti and stir gently to avoid it sticking together.

11. Allow to simmer for 12–15 minutes.

12. Drain, reserve and keep warm.

13. Taste the tomato sauce for seasoning and adjust if required.

14. Serve the spaghetti with the patties and sauce as desired.

Key cookery processes and techniques
Chopping/mixing/shaping/shallow frying/boiling/simmering

Tips
When dividing the mixture, start by dividing into two then keep dividing each amount into two thereafter until you have the required amount – for this recipe, 2 pieces per portion would suffice. Drain the patties well to prevent the sauce from being oily.

Alternative ways in which to enhance the dish
Finely chopped spring onion could be added to the mince mixture to give a different flavour.
Instead of beef, try using minced chicken or lamb.

For a healthier approach, use wholemeal breadcrumbs. The passatta could be switched for chopped tomatoes.

Ideas for garnishing
Sprinkle the dish with freshly chopped parsley to give a nice colour and flavour. Serve with crispy garlic bread and parmesan cheese.

Links to the content of following courses
Hospitality Practical Cookery Int1/Hospitality Skills for Work Int1/Home Economics Standard Grade

Basque chicken

2 portions	4 portions	Ingredients
2	4	chicken legs
250 g	500 g	red and yellow peppers
2	4	garlic cloves
100 g	200 g	ham, sliced
150 g	300 g	onion
5 g	10 g	parsley
25 ml	50 ml	vegetable oil
400 g	800 g	tomatoes, tinned
		seasoning

Preparation and cooking time – 60 minutes

1. Preheat the oven to 190 °C/375 °F/gas mark 5.

2. Cut each chicken leg into two pieces, remove the bone and cut the flesh in two.

3. Cut the peppers into 1 cm strips, roughly chop the garlic, cut the ham into 1 cm squares, dice the onion and roughly chop the parsley.

4. Heat half the oil in a pan and when hot add the chicken pieces.

5. Brown well, remove onto kitchen paper to absorb any excess oil and then place in an ovenproof dish.

6. Add the peppers, garlic, ham and seasoning.

7. Cover and cook in the oven for 20 minutes.

8. Heat the pan with the remaining oil, add the onion and cook for 5 minutes until soft.

9. Add the tomatoes, bring to the boil and simmer for 10 minutes.

10. Blend the sauce and season to taste.

11. Remove the dish from the oven, pour over the sauce and sprinkle on the parsley.

Key cookery processes and techniques
Cutting/chopping/dicing/shallow frying/ simmering/blending

Tips
When preparing the chicken leg, cut between the thigh and the drumstick to get the two pieces.

Alternative ways in which to enhance the dish
Use red instead of white onions to give more colour to the dish. Serve with braised rice; this can be cooked in the oven at the same time as the chicken.

Ideas for garnishing
Use sliced or whole black or green olives to finish the dish.

Links to the content of following courses
Hospitality Practical Cookery Int2/Hospitality Skills for Work Int2/Hospitality General Operations Int2

Energy	408 kcal
Fat	19.11 g / 3.33 g saturated
Carbohydrate	20.0 g / 17.13 g sugar
Protein	40.2 g
Fibre	4.7 g

10 Chicken chow mein

Preparation and cooking time – 30 minutes

2 portions	4 portions	Ingredients
150 g	300 g	chicken breast fillets
½	1	red pepper
½	1	spring onion
75 g	150 g	egg noodles, medium
dash		soy sauce, dark
2.5 ml	5 ml	five-spice powder
7.5 ml	15 ml	cornflour
12.5 ml	25 ml	groundnut oil
75 g	150 g	bean sprouts
12.5 ml	25 ml	soy sauce, light
dash		sesame oil
		seasoning

1. Cut the chicken into bite sized strips, the red pepper into a dice and slice the spring onion.

2. Cook the noodles in a pan of boiling water for 2–3 minutes until al dente, or according to packet instructions. Drain, then rinse under cold running water and drain again. Drizzle with a dash of sesame oil and toss through to prevent the noodles from sticking to each other.

3. Place the chicken strips in a bowl and season with a dash of dark soy sauce and the five-spice powder. Mix well, then lightly dust the chicken strips with the cornflour.

4. Heat a wok until smoking and add the groundnut oil. Carefully add the chicken and stir fry for 3–4 minutes, or until the chicken is golden-brown and cooked through.

5. Add the red pepper and stir fry for one minute, then add the bean sprouts and spring onion and stir fry for 30 seconds. Stir in the cooked noodles and season with the light soy sauce, a dash of sesame oil and pepper.

6. Pile the mixture neatly onto a serving plate and serve immediately.

Key cookery processes and techniques
Cutting/dicing/slicing/boiling/tossing/mixing/stir frying

Tips
Be careful not to overheat the wok – the food will burn very easily as the wok is so thin the heat transfers very quickly.

Alternative ways in which to enhance the dish
To give the dish a kick, you could add some chilli sauce to the noodles.

Ideas for garnishing
Chop some flat leaf parsley and coriander at the last minute and stir this through to garnish the dish.

Links to the content of following courses
Hospitality Practical Cookery Int1/Hospitality Skills for Work Int1/Home Economics Standard Grade

Energy	337 kcal
Fat	11.82 g / 2.61 g saturated
Carbohydrate	35.2 g / 4.12 g sugar
Protein	24.6 g
Fibre	2.4 g

11 Shepherd's pie

Preparation and cooking time – 90 minutes

2 portions	4 portions	Ingredients
1	2	onions
40 g	80 g	carrots
40 g	80 g	turnip
450 g	900 g	potatoes
15 ml	30 ml	oil
200 g	400 g	lamb, minced
7.5 ml	15 ml	flour
1	2	Worcester sauce, dashes
150 ml	300 ml	stock
7.5 ml	15 ml	tomato puree
2.5 ml	5 ml	parsley
		seasoning

Energy	476 kcal
Fat	19.49 g / 6.11 g saturated
Carbohydrate	52.1 g / 9.04 g sugar
Protein	26.3 g
Fibre	5.2 g

1. Preheat the oven to 200 °C/400 °F/gas mark 6.

2. Finely chop the parsley, onion and cut the carrots and turnip into a small dice. Peel the potatoes, cut into small even sized pieces and reserve.

3. Pour the olive oil into a pan on a medium heat, add the onions and shallow fry for about 5 minutes, turning the onions frequently until they start to turn brown.

4. Add the carrots and turnip and cook for a further 5 minutes turning the mix frequently. Remove them from the pan and keep them on a plate for use later.

5. Add the lamb to the pan (you may need to do this in two batches) and keep stirring and turning the meat until it is browned. Break up any pieces of the mince which are stuck together.

6. Sprinkle on the flour and mix well.

7. Add the vegetables, parsley, Worcester sauce, stock and tomato puree.

8. Turn the heat down to low, put a lid on the pan and let the mix cook for about 30 minutes.

9. Cook the potatoes, drain well and then leave them to stand for 5 minutes with no lid on the pan.

10. Mash the potatoes to a puree and season to taste.

11. Pour the mince into the base of an ovenproof dish; just over half deep is ideal.

12. Spoon the mashed potato carefully and evenly over the meat.

13. Put the dish in the preheated oven and cook for 30 minutes turning the dish round once after 15 minutes.

14. The pie is ready when the top is a golden brown.

Key cookery processes and techniques
Chopping/peeling/shallow frying/browning/
mixing/boiling/mashing/baking

Tips
Stir the mince every 10 minutes and add a couple
of tablespoons of stock/water if the mix is starting
to stick to the pan. When spooning on the mashed
potato, don't use too much pressure or it will
disappear into the meat rather than staying on top
of it – a small amount of mash at a time works
best. This dish can be prepared over two days by
cooking the mince mixture in advance.

Alternative ways in which to enhance the dish
You can add butter when mashing the potatoes to
give extra richness and flavour. Minted peas make a
great accompaniment for this dish.

Ideas for garnishing
Sprinkle grated cheese on top to give a different
taste and colour to the finished dish.

Links to the content of following courses
Hospitality Practical Cookery Int1/Hospitality
Skills for Work Int1/Home Economics Standard
Grade

 # Minced beef lasagne

Preparation and cooking time – 60 minutes

2 portions	4 portions	Ingredients
½	1	red onion
½	1	garlic clove
7.5 ml	15 ml	oil
250 g	500 g	beef, lean minced
7.5 ml	15 ml	tomato puree
200 g	400 g	tomatoes, chopped
2.5 ml	5 ml	mixed herbs
250 ml	500 ml	beef stock
10 g	20 g	margarine
10 g	20 g	flour
150 ml	300 ml	milk
50 g	100 g	Cheddar cheese, grated
2–3	4–6	lasagne sheets

1. Cut the onion into a fine dice and crush and chop the garlic.

2. Heat the oil in a pan and sweat the onion for 2 minutes. Add the garlic and continue to cook for a further minute.

3. Break the mince into the pan and colour.

4. Add the tomato puree, chopped tomatoes, mixed herbs and stock. Bring to the boil and allow to simmer whilst making the cheese sauce.

5. Melt the margarine in a pan and add the flour. Mix well and gradually stir in the milk. Bring to the boil, stirring continuously and reduce to a simmer. Cook out for 5 minutes, add the cheese and season to taste.

6. Preheat the oven to 175 °C/350 °F/gas mark 4.

7. Taste the mince and season if required.

8. Layer the mince, pasta and cheese sauce alternately in an ovenproof dish, making sure that a layer of cheese sauce is on the top.

9. Bake in the oven for 20–30 minutes.

Key cookery processes and techniques
Cutting/dicing/chopping/sweating/boiling/simmering/melting/mixing/layering

Tips
Finish with grated cheese 5 minutes before removing from the oven to give a nice colour/flavour.

Alternative ways in which to enhance the dish
Add mushrooms and mustard to the sauce to give texture and a different flavour.

Ideas for garnishing
Serve with crusty bread, rocket salad and some freshly milled black pepper.

Links to the content of following courses
Hospitality Practical Cookery Int1/Hospitality Skills for Work Int1/Home Economics Standard Grade

Energy	541 kcal
Fat	29.46 g / 12.52 g saturated
Carbohydrate	29.9 g / 10.15 g sugar
Protein	41.0 g
Fibre	2.2 g

13 Filipino pork spring rolls

Preparation and cooking time – 40 minutes

2 portions	4 portions	Ingredients
¼	½	onion, medium
¼	½	carrot
½	1	garlic clove
150 g	300 g	pork, minced
50 g	100 g	beef, minced
10 ml	20 ml	soy sauce
		seasoning
4	8	spring roll wrappers

1. Cut the onion into a fine dice, grate the carrot and crush and purée the garlic.

2. In a large bowl, combine the pork, beef, onion, carrot and garlic.

3. Gradually blend in the soy sauce and season well with pepper.

4. Lay out a wrapper on a flat surface and place about 2 tablespoons of the filling in a line down the centre.

5. Take the bottom and top edges of the wrapper and fold them towards the centre.

6. Take the left and right sides, and fold them towards the centre.

7. Moisten the last edge of the wrapper to seal.

8. Now repeat using the rest of the wrappers and filling.

9. Heat the oil in a deep fat fryer to 190 °C/375 °F.

10. Fry four spring rolls at a time for about 3 or 4 minutes, turning once.

11. The rolls are cooked through when they float, and the wrapper is a nice golden brown colour.

12. Drain onto kitchen paper, cut in half, or serve whole.

Key cookery processes and techniques
Cutting/dicing/grating/puréeing/filling/deep frying

Tips
Make sure the filling is no thicker than your thumb, or the wrapper will cook faster than the meat. Check that the oil is hot enough by adding a small piece of food first, ideally a piece of bread.

Alternative ways in which to enhance the dish
Mince the vegetables to give a smoother filling.

Ideas for garnishing
A light soya based dipping sauce made from light soya sauce and toasted sesame seeds would work well with the rolls.

Links to the content of following courses
Hospitality Practical Cookery Int2/Hospitality Skills for Work Int2/Hospitality General Operations Int2

Energy	358 kcal
Fat	20.67 g / 3.87 g saturated
Carbohydrate	19.7 g / 7.24 g sugar
Protein	23.7 g
Fibre	1.0 g

 Sausages and mash

Preparation and cooking time – 45 minutes

2 portions	4 portions	Ingredients
400 g	800 g	Maris Piper potatoes
1	2	onions
1	2	cloves garlic
50 g	100 g	butter
2.5 ml	5 ml	oil
2.5 ml	5 ml	sugar
2.5 ml	5 ml	fresh thyme
300 ml	600 ml	beef stock
4	8	pork sausages
50 ml	100 ml	milk
		seasoning

1. Peel the potatoes and cut into even sized pieces.

2. Cook the potatoes for 20 minutes in a pan of lightly salted, boiling water.

3. Slice the onions thinly and chop the garlic.

4. Warm half of the butter and the oil in a pan over a medium heat and add the onions and garlic.

5. Cook for 4 minutes stirring occasionally.

6. Preheat the grill.

7. Add the sugar to the pan and cook for a further 2 minutes.

8. Add the thyme and beef stock and reduce by four-fifths.

9. Grill the sausages, turning frequently to ensure even cooking and colouring.

10. When the potatoes are cooked, drain well, season with salt and pepper and add the remaining butter and milk.

11. Mash together until smooth.

12. To serve, place the sausages on warm serving plates with the mashed potatoes and serve with the gravy sauce.

Key cookery processes and techniques
Peeling/cutting/boiling/slicing/chopping/reducing/grilling/mashing

Tips
When cooking the sausages, take care not to have the grill at a very high heat as they will burn quickly, spoiling both the appearance and flavour.

Alternative ways in which to enhance the dish
Try using different flavours/types of sausages.

Ideas for garnishing
Mix some chopped parsley through the mash to give a nice contrasting colour. Top the dish with some lightly fried onions to complement it.

Links to the content of following courses
Hospitality Practical Cookery Int1/Hospitality Skills for Work Int1/Home Economics Standard Grade

Energy	651 kcal
Fat	39.39 g / 16.77 g saturated
Carbohydrate	51.0 g / 9.37 g sugar
Protein	26.3 g
Fibre	3.7 g

1 Leek flan

Preparation and cooking time – 70 minutes

2 portions	4 portions	Ingredients
125 g	250 g	wholemeal flour
65 g	125 g	margarine
½	1	egg yolk
		water
pinch		salt
75 g	150 g	leek, white part
20 g	40 g	butter
7.5 ml	15 ml	wholemeal flour
60 ml	120 ml	cream
30 g	60 g	Gruyère cheese
pinch		cayenne pepper

1. Preheat the oven to 200 °C/400 °F/gas mark 6.

2. Sift the flour into a bowl and rub in the margarine.

3. Make a well in the middle; add the egg yolk and two tablespoons of water.

4. Season with salt, mix together with your fingertips and then knead gently into a dough. Cover and allow to relax before use, preferably in the refrigerator.

5. Cut the leek into small, thin strips.

6. Roll out the pastry on a floured worktop to a thickness of 4 mm, line a flan tin with the pastry and bake blind in the centre of the oven for about 20 minutes.

7. Melt the butter in a pan and cook the leeks for about 5 minutes until they are transparent.

8. Sprinkle with the wholemeal flour and stir briefly.

9. Stir in the cream and two-thirds of the cheese and remove from the heat.

10. Increase the oven temperature to 245 °C/475 °F/ gas mark 9.

11. Pour the filling into the pastry case and sprinkle with last of the cheese.

12. Bake in the centre of the oven for about 15 minutes until golden brown.

Key cookery processes and techniques
Kneading/chilling/cutting/rolling/baking

Tips
The time taken to prepare this dish can be reduced by using pre-prepared pastry.

Alternative ways in which to enhance the dish
Serve with pear chutney, which would provide a sharp contrast to the flan.

Ideas for garnishing
Serve with oven baked potato wedges and crème fraîche dip.

Links to the content of following courses
Hospitality Practical Cookery Int1/Hospitality Skills for Work Int1/Home Economics Standard Grade

Energy	718 kcal
Fat	50.68 g / 22.75 g saturated
Carbohydrate	55.2 g / 4.34 g sugar
Protein	13.7 g
Fibre	5.0 g

Greek spinach
and feta filo tart

Preparation and cooking time – 60 minutes

2 portions	4 portions	Ingredients
2	4	spring onions
1	2	cloves garlic
15 ml	30 ml	olive oil
200 g	400 g	spinach leaves, young, washed
2	4	eggs, large
100 g	200 g	feta cheese
pinch		grated nutmeg
2	4	filo pastry sheets
40 g	75 g	butter, melted
		seasoning

Energy	541 kcal
Fat	41.69 g / 19.69 g saturated
Carbohydrate	15.0 g / 3.4 g sugar
Protein	21.6 g
Fibre	2.9 g

1. Preheat the oven to 190 °C/375 °F/gas mark 5.

2. Slice the spring onions and crush the garlic.

3. Heat the oil in a large pan, add the onion and garlic and sauté for 2 minutes. Add the spinach, cover with a lid and cook for 1 minute or until the leaves are wilted.

4. Transfer to a sieve and press out the excess juices.

5. Beat the eggs and crumble the cheese.

6. Add the eggs, cheese, nutmeg, a little salt and plenty of freshly ground black pepper to the spinach then mix well.

7. Brush the inside of an individual pastry mould with butter.

8. Brush the filo pastry sheets all over with melted butter.

9. Lay the first sheet of pastry down in the mould, pressing it into the base and sides. Place the second sheet on top at 90 degrees — the pastry will overhang the mould quite a lot.

10. Spoon the filling into the pastry lined mould.

11. Fold over the overlapping pastry, brushing with more butter as necessary.

12. Brush the top with the remaining butter.

13. Bake for 30–40 minutes until the pastry is golden brown and crisp.

14. Remove from the oven and cover with a tea towel for 5 minutes.

15. Serve warm or cold with salad.

Key cookery processes and techniques
Slicing/crushing/sautéing/beating/filling/baking

Tips
Always cover the uncooked filo when using it as it has a tendency to dry out. For more tips on working with filo pastry see Apple Strudel instructions on page 114.

Alternative ways in which to enhance the dish
Adding sun dried tomatoes and black olives will give the dish a different flavour.

Ideas for garnishing
Garnish with finely shredded, sautéd spring cabbage or a green salad sprinkled with sumac, a Mediterranean spice.

Links to the content of following courses
Hospitality Practical Cookery Int2/Hospitality Skills for Work Int2/Hospitality General Operations Int2

 # Onion tarte tatin

Preparation and cooking time – 70 minutes

2 portions	4 portions	Ingredients
300 g	600 g	shallots
25 g	50 g	butter
15 ml	30 ml	olive oil
40 g	75 g	brown sugar
25 ml	45 ml	balsamic vinegar
40 ml	75 ml	water
35 g	75 g	wholemeal flour
65 g	125 g	plain flour
10 ml	20 ml	French mustard
30 g	60 g	butter, for pastry
½	1	egg yolk
5 g	10 g	butter, for greasing mould
		seasoning

Energy	636 kcal
Fat	46.23 g / 24.37 g saturated
Carbohydrate	51.6 g / 28.77 g sugar
Protein	7.2 g
Fibre	4.9 g

1. Preheat the oven to 200 °C/400 °F/gas mark 6.

2. Peel the shallots, leaving them whole.

3. Put the butter and oil in a pan, add the shallots and cook over a low heat for 10 minutes, stirring often to coat the shallots with the fat.

4. Add the sugar, vinegar, four-fifths of the water and season. Stir and simmer for 20 minutes, during which time the liquid will reduce and become sticky.

5. Make the pastry by mixing together the flours, mustard, butter and egg yolk. Add the remaining water to make a dough.

6. Gather the dough into a ball, cover and refrigerate until use.

7. Butter your pastry mould, lay on the onions and pour over the sugar and vinegar liquid.

8. Roll out your dough on a piece of greaseproof paper.

9. Place the pastry on top of the onions and peel off the paper. Slightly press the pastry into the onions.

10. Cook in the oven for 25 minutes or until golden brown.

11. Remove from the oven and allow to cool for 5 minutes.

12. Place a plate on top of the tart and then turn over and remove the mould.

13. Slice and serve whilst still warm.

Key cookery processes and techniques
Peeling/simmering/reducing/mixing/rolling/
baking

Tips
Soaking the shallots in hot water for
10–15 minutes makes them easier to peel –
remember to leave the root on as this will keep the
shallot intact. The time taken to complete this dish
can be reduced by having the shallots peeled
beforehand and pastry pre-prepared.

Alternative ways in which to enhance the dish
Instead of shallots, use button onions for a
different finish. Add some fresh thyme to the sugar
mixture to give a contrasting flavour.

Ideas for garnishing
A chive cream cheese makes a lovely
accompaniment when garnishing.

Links to the content of following courses
Hospitality Practical Cookery Int2/Hospitality
Skills for Work Int2/Hospitality General Operations
Int2

Potato and vegetable frittata

Preparation and cooking time – 30 minutes

2 portions	4 portions	Ingredients
25 g	50 g	spring onions
½	1	garlic clove
25 g	50 g	green pepper
50 g	100 g	squash
100 g	200 g	potatoes
50 g	100 g	tomatoes
5 ml	10 ml	vegetable oil
3	6	eggs
pinch		mixed herbs
25 g	50 g	mozzarella cheese, grated
		seasoning

1. Slice the spring onions thinly, crush the garlic and dice the pepper very small.

2. Dice the squash and potatoes, place in seasoned cold water, bring to the boil and simmer until soft. Refresh in cold water.

3. Dice the tomatoes.

4. Heat the oil in a frying pan (make sure it has an ovenproof handle), add the onion, garlic and pepper and sweat until soft.

5. Add the squash and potatoes and continue to cook for 2–3 minutes.

6. Add the tomatoes and allow to warm through.

7. Heat the grill.

8. Beat the eggs with the mixed herbs and season.

9. Pour over the vegetable mixture and cook gently on the cooker until the eggs start to set.

10. Sprinkle on the cheese and finish cooking under the grill until a golden colour.

Key cookery processes and techniques
Slicing/crushing/dicing/simmering/sweating/beating/grilling

Tips
When you add the egg, make sure that you keep the mixture moving to prevent it from sticking fast to the pan.

Alternative ways in which to enhance the dish
You could add black olives and use red onions instead of spring onions to alter the dish.

Ideas for garnishing
A dressed micro salad with cherry tomatoes and chives gives a contrasting colour and flavour to this dish.

Links to the content of following courses
Hospitality Practical Cookery Int1/Hospitality Skills for Work Int1/Home Economics Standard Grade

Energy	243 kcal
Fat	15.08 g / 4.9 g saturated
Carbohydrate	12.0 g / 2.76 g sugar
Protein	15.7 g
Fibre	1.6 g

 # Mushroom and garlic bruschetta

Preparation and cooking time – 40 minutes

2 portions	4 portions	Ingredients
1	2	shallots
1	2	garlic cloves
125 g	250 g	button mushrooms
5 g	10 g	chives, fresh
5 ml	10 ml	vegetable oil
20 ml	45 ml	water
100 g	200 g	crème fraîche, half fat
5 ml	5 ml	vinegar
2	4	eggs, large
2	4	ciabatta bread, sliced

1. Finely dice the shallots, crush the garlic, cut the mushrooms in half and snip the chives.

2. Heat the oil in a pan, add the shallots and garlic and cook for 2–3 minutes or until soft.

3. Add the mushrooms and cook for a further 3 minutes or until the juices have come out of the mushrooms.

4. Increase the heat, add the water and cook over a high heat until the liquid has evaporated. Stir in the crème fraîche and season to taste. Gently reheat until hot and set aside.

5. Meanwhile, bring a large frying pan of lightly salted water to the boil and add the vinegar.

6. Carefully crack each of the eggs into a saucer, then tip gently into the simmering water. Poach for 3–4 minutes or until the eggs are cooked to your liking.

7. Lift the eggs from the water with a slotted spoon and drain onto kitchen paper to get rid of all the excess moisture.

8. Lightly toast the bread, then top with the mushroom mixture.

9. Place a poached egg on top and serve garnished with fresh chives.

Key cookery processes and techniques
Dicing/crushing/cutting/sautéing/poaching/toasting

Tips
The vinegar helps the egg hold its shape when cooking. Use white vinegar to keep the eggs a nice colour.

Alternative ways in which to enhance the dish
Use wild mushrooms when in season instead of the button mushrooms to give a different flavour.

Ideas for garnishing
Garnish with a rasher of baked or grilled cured ham and serve with a red onion and tomato salad.

Links to the content of following courses
Hospitality Practical Cookery Int2/Hospitality Skills for Work Int2/Hospitality General Operations Int2

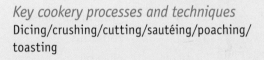

Energy	358 kcal
Fat	19.51 g / 7.8 g saturated
Carbohydrate	31.1 g / 4.91 g sugar
Protein	16.6 g
Fibre	2.4 g

6 Tabouleh

Preparation and cooking time – 40 minutes		
2 portions	**4 portions**	**Ingredients**
15 ml	30 ml	parsley
½	1	courgette
1	2	spring onions
1	2	tomatoes, blanched
5 ml	10 ml	mint leaves
15 g	30 g	dates, stoned
25 g	50 g	pine nuts
25 g	50 g	sultanas
5 ml	10 ml	mixed spice powder
2.5 ml	5 ml	ground cloves
2.5 ml	5 ml	ground star anise
250 g	500 g	couscous
10 ml	20 ml	olive oil
		seasoning

1. Finely chop the parsley, cut the courgette into a small dice, slice the spring onions finely, deseed and cut the tomato into a small dice, chop the mint and cut the dates into small, even sized pieces.

2. Preheat the grill and toast the pine nuts until they are golden in colour then set aside to cool.

3. In a bowl, mix together the parsley, courgette, spring onions, tomato, mint, dates and sultanas.

4. Boil water and pour over the couscous to rehydrate it, allowing it to stand for 5–8 minutes.

5. Remove any excess water and then mix through the spices along with some seasoning.

6. Add the olive oil and coat the granules.

7. Add the rest of the ingredients and season to taste.

Key cookery processes and techniques
Chopping/dicing/slicing/grilling/mixing

Tips
This dish can be served cold and leaving it overnight will give the flavours a chance to intensify.

Alternative ways in which to enhance the dish
Tender cuts of meat, e.g. fillet of pork or cured sausage, can be added to the dish to give a meat-based alternative.

Ideas for garnishing
Save some of the parsley and mint leaves and use as a garnish.

Links to the content of following courses
Hospitality Practical Cookery Int2/Hospitality Skills for Work Int2/Hospitality General Operations Int2

Energy	485 kcal
Fat	15.38 g / 1.41 g saturated
Carbohydrate	81.1 g / 16.88 g sugar
Protein	10.5 g
Fibre	1.7 g

Spiced vegetable biryani

Preparation and cooking time – 45 minutes

2 portions	4 portions	Ingredients
½	1	cauliflower, small
1	2	sweet potatoes
½	1	onion
½	1	red chilli
1	2	lemons
15 ml	30 ml	vegetable oil
500 ml	1 l	vegetable stock
25 g	50 g	madras curry paste
15 ml	30 ml	mustard seeds
250 g	500 g	basmati rice
25 g	50 g	peas, cooked
		seasoning

1. Preheat the oven to 215 °C/425 °F/gas mark 7.

2. Break the cauliflower into small florets, peel and dice the sweet potato, half and slice the onion thinly, deseed and finely chop the chilli and juice the lemons.

3. Pour the oil into an ovenproof dish and place in the oven to heat through for 2 minutes.

4. Carefully add the cauliflower, sweet potato and onion, ensuring that they are all coated in oil, and season well.

5. Roast in the oven for 15 minutes until they begin to brown.

6. Heat the stock and add the curry paste, chilli and mustard seeds.

7. Mix the rice with the vegetables in a pan and then carefully pour over the stock.

8. Bring the mixture to the boil.

9. Put back into the oven dish carefully.

10. Lower the oven to 190 °C/375 °F/gas mark 5, cover the dish with tin foil and braise until the rice has absorbed the liquid; this will take about 20 minutes.

11. Remove from the oven, stir in the peas and lemon juice and season to taste.

Key cookery processes and techniques
Peeling/dicing/slicing/roasting/braising

Tips
When removing the ovenproof dish from the oven, remember to place it either on top of the cooker or on a stand that will protect your work surface from the intense heat.

Alternative ways in which to enhance the dish
The main vegetables in the dish can be replaced by seasonal vegetables or vegetables of your liking – just make sure that they are not too firm a vegetable, e.g. carrots, and that you prepare them so they will all cook in the same time.

Ideas for garnishing
Cashew nuts and coriander could be used to finish the dish, the nuts adding texture and the herb colour.

Links to the content of following courses
Hospitality Practical Cookery Int2/Hospitality Skills for Work Int2/Hospitality General Operations Int2

Energy	657 kcal
Fat	13.97 g / 1.22 g saturated
Carbohydrate	130.3 g / 8.21 g sugar
Protein	14.9 g
Fibre	4.7 g

Stuffed peppers

Preparation and cooking time – 60 minutes

2 portions	4 portions	Ingredients
2	4	peppers
15 ml	30 ml	olive oil
½	1	onion
1	2	garlic cloves
200 ml	400 ml	tomatoes, tinned chopped
100 g	200 g	basmati rice
5 ml	10 ml	dried oregano
		seasoning
		boiling water

Energy	304 kcal
Fat	8.71 g / 1.25 g saturated
Carbohydrate	54.0 g / 8.76 g sugar
Protein	6.2 g
Fibre	4.1 g

1. Preheat the oven to 190 °C/375 °F/gas mark 5.
2. To prepare the peppers, cut them in half through the stalk.
3. Make sure that all the white bits inside and seeds are removed.
4. Finely dice the onion and crush the garlic.
5. In a heated frying pan, add the olive oil and the onion.
6. Cook the onion until it is soft – about 2–3 minutes.
7. Add the garlic and cook for a further minute.
8. Strain the tomato liquid into a measuring jug and make up to 300/600 ml using the already boiled water. Keep the strained tomatoes for later.
9. Add the rice and oregano to the onions and garlic in the pan. Add the tomato juice and water mixture and bring to the boil.
10. Cover the pan and let it simmer for 8 minutes.
11. Add the remaining chopped tomatoes, mix through and season to taste.
12. Remove the pan from the heat and let it settle until all the liquid has been absorbed.
13. Now take the peppers and stuff them carefully with the mixture.
14. Put the peppers in a baking tray and pour just a little water into the bottom of the tray for steaming purposes.
15. Bake the peppers uncovered in the oven for approx. 30 minutes or until the peppers are nice and soft and the rims are just lightly browned.

Key cookery processes and techniques
Cutting/dicing/crushing/sautéing/straining/
simmering/steaming

Tips
Be careful not to brown the onions as this alters
the taste.

*Alternative ways in which to enhance the
dish*
Use wild rice for a healthy option and remember
that wild rice takes longer to cook.

Ideas for garnishing
Carefully arrange the pepper half neatly on the
plate to show the filling. Serve with salad leaves,
julienne of beetroot and carrot ribbons tossed in a
low fat dressing.

Links to the content of following courses
Hospitality Practical Cookery Int2/Hospitality
Skills for Work Int2/Hospitality General Operations
Int2

9 Chickpea cutlet

Preparation and cooking time – 40 minutes

2 portions	4 portions	Ingredients
4	8	basil leaves
½	1	garlic clove
200 g	400 g	chickpeas, cooked
30 ml	60 ml	oat bran
30 ml	60 ml	porridge oats
100 g	200 g	brown rice, cooked
100 g	200 g	tofu, firm
40 ml	75 ml	barbecue sauce
10 ml	20 ml	vegetable oil
		seasoning

1. Chop the basil leaves and crush the garlic.

2. In a bowl, mash the chickpeas and basil together.

3. Mix in the bran, oats and rice – the mixture will be dry.

4. In a separate bowl, mash the tofu and drain off any excess water.

5. Add the garlic and barbecue sauce to the tofu and mix well.

6. Mix together the chickpeas and tofu and season well.

7. Shape into cutlets and reserve.

8. Heat the oil in a large frying pan and cook the cutlets for 5 minutes each side, taking care not to over colour them.

Energy	351 kcal
Fat	12.01 g / 1.31 g saturated
Carbohydrate	48.6 g / 5.24 g sugar
Protein	15.0 g
Fibre	6.6 g

Key cookery processes and techniques
Chopping/crushing/mashing/mixing/shaping/shallow frying

Tips
Use a palette knife to help shape the cutlets. Use a fish slice to turn the cutlets whilst they are cooking to prevent them from falling apart.

Alternative ways in which to enhance the dish
The bran and oats can be toasted first to give a different flavour.

Ideas for garnishing
Serve the cutlets in warm buns along with a fresh seasonal salad and natural yoghurt flavoured with garlic and cucumber.

Links to the content of following courses
Hospitality Practical Cookery Int1/Hospitality Skills for Work Int1/Home Economics Standard Grade

CHAPTER 4

Desserts

Chocolate roulade with white chocolate and orange sauce

Preparation and cooking time – 75 minutes

2 portions	4 portions	Ingredients
60 g	120 g	plain chocolate
2	4	eggs
60 g	120 g	caster sugar
75 ml	150 ml	whipping cream
10 ml	20 ml	icing sugar
½	1	orange, zest
50 g	100 g	white chocolate
50 ml	100 ml	double cream
50 ml	100 ml	milk

Energy	813 kcal
Fat	51.72 g / 29.61 g saturated
Carbohydrate	77.8 g / 77.5 g sugar
Protein	14.1 g
Fibre	2.0 g

1. Preheat the oven to 180 °C/360 °F/gas mark 4.

2. Grease a Swiss roll baking tin and line with grease proof paper.

3. Melt the plain chocolate in a heatproof bowl set over a pan of hot water. Separate the eggs.

4. Whisk the egg whites to form a peak, and reserve in the refrigerator.

5. Whisk the egg yolks and caster sugar until light and cream coloured.

6. Whisk in the warmed, melted chocolate then loosen with a spoonful of the egg white.

7. Add the remaining egg white gently and pour into the prepared baking tin.

8. Bake for 20 minutes, cool for 5 minutes then turn the cake out onto sugared greaseproof paper.

9. Peel the paper from the roulade, trim the edges then cover with greaseproof and a damp towel. Leave for 30 minutes to cool.

10. Whip the whipping cream and icing sugar to a soft peak then spread over the roulade.

11. Roll up into a cylinder shape using the paper, tying the ends to secure the shape, and chill until required.

12. Melt the white chocolate in a heatproof bowl set over a pan of hot water.

13. Zest the orange.

14. Pour the double cream and milk into a small, heavy-based pan and heat until scalding hot but not quite boiling.

15. Remove from the heat and mix into the white chocolate, whisking constantly to make a smooth sauce.

16. Add the orange zest.

17. Serve the roulade in slices with a spoonful of the sauce to the side.

Key cookery processes and techniques
Melting/whisking/baking/whipping/zesting

Tips
Do not let the bottom of the bowl touch the water when melting the chocolate as the heat will be too intense and will make the chocolate unworkable. Also, remember that white chocolate is harder to cook with, as it is more unstable.

Alternative ways in which to enhance the dish
The orange zest could be simply added to crème fraîche to provide a healthier sauce to complement the dish.

Ideas for garnishing
A sprig of fresh mint leaves could be used to finish of the dish.

Links to the content of following courses
Hospitality Practical Cookery Int2/Hospitality Skills for Work Int2/Hospitality General Operations Int2

 # Coffee and mascarpone tiramisu

Preparation and cooking time – 45 minutes

2 portions	4 portions	Ingredients
25 g	50 g	sugar
7.5 ml	15 ml	coffee powder
65 ml	125 ml	boiling water
½	1	gelatine, pre-soaked leaf
25 ml	50 ml	whipping cream
5 g	10 g	icing sugar
15 g	25 g	mascarpone cheese
6	12	amaretto biscuits
5 g	10 g	chocolate, grated
		cocoa powder, to dust

1. Add the sugar and coffee to the boiling water and boil again until the sugar has dissolved.

2. Add the gelatine and allow to cool slightly.

3. Whip the cream and sweeten with the icing sugar.

4. When the coffee syrup has cooled slightly, beat half into the mascarpone cheese.

5. Fold in the cream.

6. Place a layer of the biscuits in the bottom of a dish.

7. Spoon some of the remaining syrup over.

8. Pipe or spoon half of the cream mixture over the biscuits.

9. Repeat the process so that the dish is topped with cream.

10. Decorate with the grated chocolate and dust with cocoa.

Key cookery processes and techniques
Boiling/whipping/beating/folding in/piping/grating

Tips
Assemble the dish near to service so that the biscuits are still a little crisp.

Alternative ways in which to enhance the dish
For a stronger flavour, use fresh coffee instead of coffee powder.

Ideas for garnishing
Serve with chocolate shapes and some of the biscuits.

Links to the content of following courses
Hospitality Practical Cookery Int1/Hospitality Skills for Work Int1/Home Economics Standard Grade

Energy	214 kcal
Fat	9.04 g / 5.58 g saturated
Carbohydrate	31.8 g / 26.55 g sugar
Protein	13.6 g
Fibre	0.3 g

Truffle cake

Preparation and cooking time – 40 minutes,
4 hours setting time

2 portions	4 portions	Ingredients
		chocolate and vanilla sponge, cut into a 1 cm thick disc
20 ml	40 ml	water
12.5 g	25 g	brown sugar
dash		rum essence
100 g	200 g	plain chocolate
150 ml	300 ml	double cream
1	2	egg yolks
25 g	50 g	caster sugar
Topping		
25 g	50 g	milk chocolate
12.5 ml	25 ml	double cream
7.5 g	15 g	unsalted butter

1. Place the sponge into the bottom of lined individual rings or a flan ring.

2. For the rum syrup, boil the water with the brown sugar until it is dissolved then add the rum essence to taste.

3. For the cake, melt the plain chocolate with half the cream in a bowl set over hot water.

4. Whisk the egg yolks and sugar until pale and fluffy.

5. Whip the remaining cream to a soft peak.

6. Spoon some syrup over the sponge, taking care not to use too much.

7. Once the chocolate has melted, remove from the heat and beat in the egg mixture.

8. Fold the whipped cream into the chocolate mixture and pour on top of the sponge in the tin.

9. Leave to set in the refrigerator for up to 4 hours.

10. To make the topping, melt the milk chocolate with the cream, add the butter and remove from the heat.

11. Leave to cool and thicken then spread over the top of the cake.

Key cookery processes and techniques
Boiling/melting/whisking/whipping/beating/folding

Tips
This dish works better when prepared in stages, with the filling being best left overnight to set.

Alternative ways in which to enhance the dish
To ensure a glossy finish, glaze each portion with a gas gun for a few seconds before serving.

Ideas for garnishing
Dust with cocoa powder or use chocolate shavings. Decorate with sliced fresh fruit.

Links to the content of following courses
Hospitality Practical Cookery Int2/Hospitality Skills for Work Int2/Hospitality General Operations Int2

Energy	853 kcal
Fat	67.32 g / 40.62 g saturated
Carbohydrate	59.7 g / 59.25 g sugar
Protein	6.2 g
Fibre	1.4 g

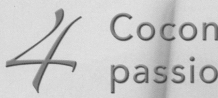

Coconut tart with passion fruit cream

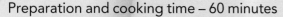

Preparation and cooking time – 60 minutes

2 portions	4 portions	Ingredients
½	1	lemon
½	1	egg
50 g	100 g	caster sugar
100 ml	200 ml	double cream
50 g	100 g	desiccated coconut
2 individual	1x10 cm	pastry case
50 g	100 g	mascarpone
50 ml	100 ml	whipping cream
25 g	50 g	icing sugar
37.5 ml	75 ml	passion fruit pulp

1. Preheat the oven to 160 °C/325 °F/gas mark 3.

2. Zest and juice the lemon.

3. Mix together the egg, lemon zest and caster sugar.

4. Gently mix in the double cream, coconut and lemon juice.

5. Pour the mixture into the pastry case and bake for 40 minutes.

6. Whip together the mascarpone, whipping cream and icing sugar.

7. As it thickens, add the passion fruit pulp and beat until firm.

8. Allow the tart to cool for an hour to firm up prior to serving.

Energy	1367 kcal
Fat	115.95 g / 77.43 g saturated
Carbohydrate	71.3 g / 56.51 g sugar
Protein	12.1 g
Fibre	12.7 g

Key cookery processes and techniques
Zesting/juicing/mixing/baking/whipping/beating/cooling

Tips
Use the mascarpone at room temperature to ensure a smooth combination. The pastry case can be made in advance, preferably the previous day.

Alternative ways in which to enhance the dish
Toast the coconut first to give a different taste to this dish.

Ideas for garnishing
Serve with the passion fruit cream and a passion fruit syrup.

Links to the content of following courses
Hospitality Practical Cookery Int1/Hospitality Skills for Work Int1/Home Economics Standard Grade

5 Likapa roll

Preparation and cooking time – 50 minutes

2 portions	4 portions	Ingredients
25 g	50 g	flour
12.5 g	25 g	cocoa powder
1½	3	eggs
37.5 g	75 g	caster sugar
30 ml	60 ml	chocolate spread
50 ml	100 ml	whipping cream
		cocoa powder for dusting

1. Preheat oven to 215 °C/425 °F/gas mark 7.

2. Grease a Swiss roll baking tin and line with greaseproof paper.

3. Whisk the eggs and sugar until very thick and creamy.

4. Sieve the flour and cocoa on top of the egg mixture and carefully fold in.

5. Pour into the prepared baking tin.

6. Bake for 8–10 minutes until golden brown and well risen.

7. Turn the sponge onto sugared greaseproof paper and trim the edges. Cover with another piece of greaseproof paper and roll up immediately. Leave to cool.

8. Whisk the cream until it stands in peaks.

9. Carefully unroll the sponge, cover with the chocolate spread and the cream.

10. Carefully re-roll and dust liberally with cocoa powder.

11. Cut into portions and serve.

Key cookery processes and techniques
Greasing/sieving/whisking/folding/baking/rolling

Tips
Prepare the tin in advance. If making two portions, fold the greaseproof paper accordingly.

Alternative ways in which to enhance the dish
Add some chopped mixed nuts on top of the filling to give a contrasting flavour and crunchy texture.

Ideas for garnishing
Decorate with piped cream and serve with a white chocolate sauce.

Links to the content of following courses
Hospitality Practical Cookery Int1/Hospitality Skills for Work Int1/Home Economics Standard Grade

Energy	384 kcal
Fat	22.13 g / 8.55 g saturated
Carbohydrate	39.4 g / 29.12 g sugar
Protein	9.3 g
Fibre	1.1 g

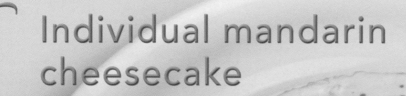

6 Individual mandarin cheesecake

Preparation and cooking time – 30 minutes

2 portions	4 portions	Ingredients
20 g	40 g	unsalted butter
50 g	100 g	digestive biscuits
75 g	150 g	tinned mandarins, drained
50 g	100 g	low fat cream cheese
10 g	20 g	icing sugar
75 ml	150 ml	double cream
		chocolate to decorate

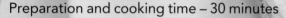

1. Melt the butter.

2. Crush the biscuits and mix with the butter.

3. Divide the mixture into individual circular moulds and push down gently to an even thickness.

4. Saving a few whole for decoration, chop the remaining mandarins.

5. Beat together the cream cheese and icing sugar.

6. Whisk the cream to a soft peak.

7. Mix the chopped mandarins, cream cheese and half of the whipped cream together gently.

8. Spoon the mixture into the moulds and allow to set in the refrigerator.

9. To serve, remove from the mould and use the remaining mandarins and some chocolate to decorate.

Energy	454 kcal
Fat	36.71 g / 22.68 g saturated
Carbohydrate	26.7 g / 13.92 g sugar
Protein	3.2 g
Fibre	0.8 g

Key cookery processes and techniques
Melting/crushing/mixing/chopping/beating/whisking

Tips
The chocolate for decoration can be simply grated or shaved using a vegetable peeler.

Alternative ways in which to enhance the dish
Any soft or cooked fruit can be used in this dish instead of the mandarins.

Ideas for garnishing
Decorate with orange or mandarin segments, chocolate sauce and a sprig of mint.

Links to the content of following courses
Hospitality Practical Cookery Int2/Hospitality Skills for Work Int2/Hospitality General Operations Int2

7 Caramel choux buns

Preparation and cooking time – 60 minutes

2 portions	4 portions	Ingredients
75 ml	150 ml	water
pinch		salt
25 g	50 g	butter
40 g	80 g	strong flour
1	2	eggs, beaten
50 ml	100 ml	whipping cream
10 g	20 g	icing sugar
12.5 g	25 g	caster sugar
10 ml	20 ml	water
62.5 ml	125 ml	double cream

1. Preheat the oven to 200 °C/400 °F/gas mark 6.

2. Bring the water and the butter to the boil, add the sifted flour and salt, and stir until smooth.

3. Allow to cool slightly then add the beaten egg. Mix well.

4. Pipe into small rounds on a lightly greased baking sheet and bake for 20–25 minutes.

5. Beat the whipping cream and icing sugar to a soft peak and reserve.

6. Bring the caster sugar and water to the boil in a pan and cook until amber in colour.

7. Remove from the heat and allow to continue to darken slightly before adding the double cream.

8. Return to the heat, bring to the boil and remove.

9. Fill choux buns with the whipped cream and serve with the caramel sauce.

Energy	481 kcal
Fat	40.67 g / 24.24 g saturated
Carbohydrate	22.9 g / 8.12 g sugar
Protein	7.3 g
Fibre	0.6 g

Key cookery processes and techniques
Boiling/sifting/stirring/beating/piping/filling

Tips
Allow the choux buns to cool before filling so that the cream does not melt or go soft.

Alternative ways in which to enhance the dish
Chocolate sauce could be used to give a different flavour.

Ideas for garnishing
Pour on the caramel sauce, add a few fresh strawberries and dust with icing sugar.

Links to the content of following courses
Hospitality Practical Cookery Int2/Hospitality Skills for Work Int2/Hospitality General Operations Int2

Chocolate tart

Preparation and cooking time – 90 minutes

2 portions	4 portions	Ingredients
20 g	40 g	softened butter
20 g	40 g	caster sugar
10 g	20 g	plain chocolate, melted and cooled
½	1	egg
50 g	100 g	plain flour
5 g	10 g	cocoa powder
pinch		salt
Filling		
50 g	100 g	plain chocolate, melted
75 ml	150 ml	double cream
25 ml	50 ml	milk
½	1	large egg
25 g	50 g	caster sugar
few drops		vanilla essence

Energy	648 kcal
Fat	41.26 g / 24.27 g saturated
Carbohydrate	63.7 g / 44.07 g sugar
Protein	9.5 g
Fibre	1.8 g

1. In a bowl, cream the butter and sugar until pale and fluffy. Mix in the melted chocolate and egg.

2. Sift the flour, cocoa powder and salt together, add to the mixture and knead lightly to a smooth dough. Shape into a flat disc, wrap in clingfilm and chill for 30 minutes.

3. Preheat the oven to 190 °C/375 °F/gas mark 5.

4. Roll out the pastry on a lightly floured board and use to line individual moulds or a flan tin (let the pastry overhang the top; chill for 15–20 minutes).

5. Prick the pastry base, then line with foil and baking beans and bake blind for 15 minutes.

6. Remove the beans and foil, trim the pastry level with the top of the tin and bake for a further 5 minutes.

7. Leave the pastry to cool and reduce the oven temperature to 150 °C/300 °F/gas mark 2.

8. For the filling, brush a third of the melted chocolate evenly over the base.

9. Bring the cream and milk to the boil in a pan, then pour into the remaining melted chocolate, stirring until smooth.

10. Whisk together the eggs, sugar and vanilla then mix with the chocolate cream.

11. Put the moulds/tin on a baking sheet on the middle oven shelf, pulled halfway out and set level. Pour in the chocolate filling, ease the shelf back in and bake for 30 minutes.

12. The filling will be wobbly, but set. Serve at room temperature.

Key cookery processes and techniques
Creaming/melting/mixing/sifting/kneading/
shaping/rolling/baking blind/whisking

Tips
Try not to heat the chocolate too much for the
pastry as it will require to be cooled for longer.
Make and bake the pastry in advance to save time.

Alternative ways in which to enhance the dish
Add some pecan nuts to the chocolate filling
mixture to give a different texture and flavour.

Ideas for garnishing
Dust the tart heavily with cocoa before serving
with some orange segments.

Links to the content of following courses
Hospitality Practical Cookery Int2/Hospitality
Skills for Work Int2/Hospitality General Operations
Int2

9 Summer pudding

Preparation and cooking time – 30 minutes

2 portions	4 portions	Ingredients
50 g	100 g	strawberries
50 g	100 g	raspberries
25 g	50 g	blackcurrants
25 g	50 g	redcurrants
35 g	70 g	caster sugar
pinch		ginger powder
pinch		cinnamon powder
4	8	white bread, slices

1. Cut the strawberries into quarters.

2. Put all the fruit and sugar into a pan and heat gently to draw out the moisture.

3. When a liquid has collected, bring to the boil, add the spices and simmer for 5 minutes.

4. Line individual moulds – start by cutting two discs of bread, a smaller one for the bottom of the mould and a larger one for the top, then cut the remaining bread into even sized strips for the side of the mould.

5. Place the smaller disc in the bottom of the mould and build round the inside of each with the strips.

6. Drain the fruit and reserve the juices.

7. Spoon the fruit into the moulds and moisten with the juice.

8. Place the larger disc of bread on top, making sure that the fruit is covered.

9. Weigh down carefully and place in the refrigerator overnight.

10. Remove the puddings from the moulds to serve.

Key cookery processes and techniques
Cutting/boiling/simmering/draining/moulding

Tips
Make sure that the bread has been well soaked; if it is dry it will not taste as nice.

Alternative ways in which to enhance the dish
Prepare in a large mould instead of individual ones and serve whole.

Ideas for garnishing
Serve with sweetened cream and fresh berries.

Links to the content of following courses
Hospitality Practical Cookery Int2/Hospitality Skills for Work Int2/Hospitality General Operations Int2

Energy	258 kcal
Fat	1.48 g / 0.32 g saturated
Carbohydrate	58.1 g / 24.32 g sugar
Protein	6.9 g
Fibre	2.9 g

10 Cranachan

Preparation and cooking time – 20 minutes

2 portions	4 portions	Ingredients
25 g	50 g	medium oatmeal
170 g	340 g	raspberries
25 g	50 g	icing sugar
125 ml	250 ml	double cream
25 ml	50 ml	heather honey

1. Toast the oatmeal under a grill, turning occasionally, until golden brown and allow to cool.

2. Mix the raspberries with the icing sugar.

3. Whip the cream until stiff.

4. Fold in the oatmeal and honey.

5. Layer the cream mixture with the raspberries in tall glasses, reserving a few raspberries for garnish.

6. Cover with cling film and refrigerate.

7. Allow to come to room temperature for 30 minutes before serving.

8. Decorate with a few raspberries.

Energy	467 kcal
Fat	34.91 g / 20.95 g saturated
Carbohydrate	36.7 g / 27.5 g sugar
Protein	3.8 g
Fibre	3.0 g

Key cookery processes and techniques
Toasting/grilling/mixing/whipping/folding/layering

Tips
Assemble as close to service as possible to leave the oatmeal crisp.

Alternative ways in which to enhance the dish
You can use any soft fruit that is in season with this dish.

Ideas for garnishing
Decorate with toasted oatmeal and mint tips.

Links to the content of following courses
Hospitality Practical Cookery Int1/Hospitality Skills for Work Int1/Home Economics Standard Grade

11 Raspberry fool

Preparation and cooking time – 30 minutes

2 portions	4 portions	Ingredients
125 g	250 g	raspberries, fresh
25 g	50 g	caster sugar
75 ml	150 ml	double cream
75 ml	150 ml	plain yoghurt
		mint leaves

1. Crush the raspberries with a stainless steel or silver fork in a china or glass bowl.

2. Mix them with the sugar and put them on one side for 10 minutes. The sugar on the raspberries will draw out juice and bright colour.

3. Beat the double cream until it is thick, then, tablespoon by tablespoon, beat the yoghurt into it.

4. Swirl the raspberry and sugar mixture into the cream and yoghurt – do not mix it so thoroughly that it looks like pink yoghurt; swirl it in so that it is marbled.

5. Pour it into glasses so you can see the marbled effect, decorate each one with a sprig of mint and put to set in the fridge for at least 30 minutes before serving.

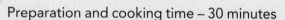

Energy	272 kcal
Fat	20.7 g / 12.83 g saturated
Carbohydrate	19.4 g / 19.3 g sugar
Protein	3.3 g
Fibre	1.6 g

Key cookery processes and techniques
Crushing/mixing/beating

Tips
The cream will not thin down if you beat it each time you put in a dollop of yoghurt, it will bulk back up again. It allows you to have twice the amount of cream, as it were, with only half the amount of fat.

Alternative ways in which to enhance the dish
Stewed rhubarb or apples make good alternatives when raspberries are out of season.

Ideas for garnishing
Fresh berries and mint tips are ideal for garnishing this dish.

Links to the content of following courses
Hospitality Practical Cookery Int1/Hospitality Skills for Work Int1/Home Economics Standard Grade

12 Bramley apple brûlée

Preparation and cooking time – 90 minutes

2 portions	4 portions	Ingredients
2	4	Bramley apples
200 ml	400 ml	single cream
1.5 ml	3 ml	cinnamon powder
pinch		ground cloves
2	4	egg yolks
25 g	50 g	caster sugar

1. Preheat the oven to 170 °C/340 °F/gas mark 4.

2. Place the apples in a small roasting pan with 1 cm of water.

3. Bake for 40 minutes until tender.

4. Remove from the oven and allow to cool a little.

5. Pour the cream into a small saucepan.

6. Almost bring to the boil then remove from the heat.

7. Scoop the flesh from the apples and place in a food processor.

8. Add the spices, egg yolks and half the sugar. Blend for 2–3 minutes until smooth.

9. Add the scalded cream and blend again.

10. Pour the mixture into ramekins.

11. Place in a bain-marie and bake for 25–30 minutes or until set. Allow to cool.

12. To serve, sprinkle with the remainder of the sugar, spray with a little water and glaze with a blow torch.

Energy	305 kcal
Fat	22 g / 12.94 g saturated
Carbohydrate	23.3 g / 23.3 g sugar
Protein	5.0 g
Fibre	1.4 g

Key cookery processes and techniques
Baking/boiling/blending/glazing

Tips
To quicken the preparation of this dish, you could have the apples already puréed. This dish works well when prepared over two days.

Alternative ways in which to enhance the dish
Pears can replace the apples in the recipe.

Ideas for garnishing
A tuille biscuit or apple crisp is a nice accompaniment to this dish, as are some lightly poached apple slices dusted with cinnamon.

Links to the content of following courses
Hospitality Practical Cookery Int2/Hospitality Skills for Work Int2/Hospitality General Operations Int2

1 Spiced apple crumble

Preparation and cooking time – 60 minutes

2 portions	4 portions	Ingredients
100 g	200 g	flour
pinch		cinnamon powder
12.5 g	25 g	mixed nuts, ground
50 g	100 g	butter
25 g	50 g	brown sugar
250 g	500 g	cooking apples
¼	½	orange, juice of
12.5 g	25 g	caster sugar

1. Preheat the oven to 200 °C/400 °F/gas mark 6.

2. Sift the flour and cinnamon into a large bowl and add the nuts. Rub in the butter using your fingertips until the mixture resembles coarse breadcrumbs. Stir in the brown sugar then place in the fridge while you prepare the apples.

3. Peel, core and cut the apples into thick slices. Tip into an ovenproof dish, add the orange juice and sugar and toss lightly.

4. Pile the crumble mixture evenly over the apples and bake for 35–40 minutes or until hot, bubbling and golden brown on top.

Key cookery processes and techniques
Sieving/rubbing in/peeling/coring/cutting/baking

Tips
You can make the crumble mixture in a food processor but take care not to over-process and make the butter pieces too small.
The apple can be par-cooked before adding the crumble mixture.

Alternative ways in which to enhance the dish
Make an oat crumble by adding 75 g coarse oats and take out the same amount of flour.
Add a few blueberries to the apple mixture to give a complementary flavour.

Ideas for garnishing
Serve with vanilla custard, single cream, or ice cream.

Links to the content of following courses
Hospitality Practical Cookery Int1/Hospitality Skills for Work Int1/Home Economics Standard Grade

Energy	503 kcal
Fat	24.2 g / 13.67 g saturated
Carbohydrate	69.6 g / 31.08 g sugar
Protein	6.9 g
Fibre	3.7 g

2 Pear and cinnamon Eve's pudding

Preparation and cooking time – 75 minutes

2 portions	4 portions	Ingredients
200 g	400 g	pears
40 g	80 g	brown sugar
¼	½	lemon, zest and juice
2.5 ml	5 ml	cinnamon powder
60 g	120 g	plain flour
¼ tsp	½ tsp	baking powder
30 g	60 g	butter
30 g	60 g	caster sugar
½	1	egg
a little		milk

1. Preheat the oven to 180 °C/360 °F/gas mark 4.

2. Peel, core and slice the pears into ½ cm slices.

3. Combine the pears, brown sugar, lemon zest and lemon juice in a pan with a little water.

4. Bring to a simmer, add the cinnamon and cook gently for about 10 minutes, or until tender.

5. Transfer the cooked pears to the base of a pie dish and set aside as you prepare the sponge.

6. Sift together the flour and baking powder into a bowl.

7. In a separate bowl cream together the butter and caster sugar until light and fluffy.

8. Add the egg and beat thoroughly to combine.

9. Lightly fold in the flour mix, adding a little milk, as needed, to form a stiff batter.

10. Spoon the sponge on top of the pears and bake for about 40–50 minutes, or until the sponge is cooked and the top is golden.

Key cookery processes and techniques
Peeling/coring/slicing/simmering/sifting/creaming/beating/folding/baking

Tips
Test to see if the sponge is cooked by pushing a sharp object – a small knife or a skewer – into the centre of it. If the knife/skewer comes out clean, the sponge will be cooked through. Buttering the dish will prevent the pudding from sticking.

Alternative ways in which to enhance the dish
Try placing the fruit into the sponge instead of covering it; this will give a different finish to the dish.

Ideas for garnishing
Serve hot with a vanilla custard sauce.

Links to the content of following courses
Hospitality Practical Cookery Int1/Hospitality Skills for Work Int1/Home Economics Standard Grade

Energy	409 kcal
Fat	14.63 g / 8.46 g saturated
Carbohydrate	68.9 g / 45.85 g sugar
Protein	5.5 g
Fibre	2.9 g

3 Apple puff pastry tart

Preparation and cooking time – 50 minutes

2 portions	4 portions	Ingredients
1	2	cooking apples
10 g	20 g	brown sugar
pinch		ginger powder
2	4	Golden Delicious apples
75 g	150 g	puff pastry
25 g	50 g	butter, melted
		caster sugar, to dredge
75 ml	150 ml	single cream
75 g	150 g	granulated sugar

1. Preheat the oven to 190 °C/375 °F/gas mark 5.

2. Peel, core and cut the cooking apple into even sized pieces.

3. Place in a pan with a little water, brown sugar and ginger powder.

4. Cook for 5 minutes or until soft enough to purée.

5. Blend to a lump-free mixture and allow to cool.

6. Peel and core the golden delicious apples then carefully slice them thinly.

7. Roll the pastry out into even sized portions, to a shape of your choice.

8. Place on a baking sheet, prick all over with a fork and spoon on some apple puree.

9. Neatly arrange the apple slices on top of the pastry.

10. Brush with the melted butter, dredge with caster sugar and bake for 15 minutes.

11. To make the caramel sauce, bring the cream and sugar to the boil, reduce to a simmer and cook out for 5–10 minutes.

12. Serve the tart warm with the caramel sauce.

Key cookery processes and techniques
Peeling/coring/cutting/puréeing/blending/slicing/rolling/baking/reducing

Tips
When using a pastry brush, never leave it soaking in the liquid as it will absorb too much. When you then use it, you'll end up putting too much liquid onto your food and end up spoiling the appearance.

Alternative ways in which to enhance the dish
Brush the finished tart with boiled apricot jam to glaze.

Ideas for garnishing
Serve with ice cream or a fresh egg custard.

Links to the content of following courses
Hospitality Practical Cookery Int2/Hospitality Skills for Work Int2/Hospitality General Operations Int2

Energy	542 kcal
Fat	26.8 g / 11.07 g saturated
Carbohydrate	77.2 g / 63.31 g sugar
Protein	4.1 g
Fibre	2.8 g

4 Clootie-less dumpling

Preparation and cooking time – 20 minutes

2 portions	4 portions	Ingredients
125 ml	250 ml	water
90 g	180 g	soft brown sugar
7.5 ml	15 ml	mixed spice powder
7.5 ml	15 ml	cinnamon powder
100 g	200 g	margarine
50 g	100 g	raisins
50 g	100 g	currants
100 g	200 g	sultanas
7.5 ml	15 ml	treacle
100 g	200 g	plain flour
½ tsp	1 tsp	bicarbonate of soda
1	2	eggs

1. Boil the water, sugar, mixed spice, cinnamon, margarine, fruit and treacle in a pan.

2. Simmer gently for 1 minute, remove from the heat.

3. Sieve the flour and bicarbonate of soda and add to the pan, mixing well.

4. Beat in the egg well when the mixture has cooled slightly.

5. Line a microwavable bowl with cling film then add the mixture.

6. Cook in the microwave at 650 W for 9 minutes.

7. Allow to stand until cool, then serve.

Energy	940 kcal
Fat	34.08 g / 7.12 g saturated
Carbohydrate	157.6 g / 119.48 g sugar
Protein	11.3 g
Fibre	3.5 g

Key cookery processes and techniques
Boiling/simmering/sieving/mixing/beating/microwaving

Tips
Leave the ingredients to sit overnight to allow the flavours to develop.

Alternative ways in which to enhance the dish
You could add chopped nuts or use only your preferred dried fruit when preparing the dumpling.

Ideas for garnishing
Serve as a dessert with ice cream or custard or as an afternoon tea item with butter, jam or clotted cream.

Links to the content of following courses
Hospitality Practical Cookery Int1/Hospitality Skills for Work Int1/Home Economics Standard Grade

5 Blueberry clafoutis

Preparation and cooking time – 40 minutes

2 portions	4 portions	Ingredients
20 g	40 g	flaked almonds, toasted
7.5 g	15 g	plain flour
pinch		salt
35 g	70 g	caster sugar
1	2	eggs
1	2	egg yolks
75 ml	150 ml	double cream
		soft butter, for buttering dishes
50 g	100 g	blueberries
		icing sugar, for dusting

1. Grind the almonds to a very fine powder in a blender then add in the flour and salt.

2. Add the sugar, the whole eggs, the yolks and cream and whisk until smooth.

3. Store in a jug and allow to rest for up to 24 hours.

4. When ready to cook, preheat the oven to 200 °C/400 °F/gas mark 6.

5. Butter 10 cm ovenproof dishes and scatter the blueberries in the bottom.

6. Give the batter a good stir and pour into the gratin dishes; bake for 18–20 minutes until risen and lightly firm.

7. Dust with icing sugar and serve.

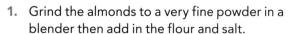

Energy	472 kcal
Fat	31.96 g / 14.76 g saturated
Carbohydrate	39.6 g / 36.45 g sugar
Protein	9.0 g
Fibre	1.3 g

Key cookery processes and techniques
Grinding/whisking/buttering/stirring/pouring/baking

Tips
Whilst the batter is best rested for up to 24 hours, it can be made and used on the same day.

Alternative ways in which to enhance the dish
Blackberries or even orange segments make a good alternative if blueberries are out of season.

Ideas for garnishing
Dust with icing sugar and serve with ice cream or fresh egg custard.

Links to the content of following courses
Hospitality Practical Cookery Int1/Hospitality Skills for Work Int1/Home Economics Standard Grade

Queen of puddings

Preparation and cooking time – 60 minutes

2 portions	4 portions	Ingredients
50 ml	100 ml	milk
50 ml	100 ml	double cream
dash		vanilla extract
25 g	50 g	caster sugar
1	2	eggs, separated
37.5 g	75 g	fresh breadcrumbs
½	1	lemon, zest
37.5 g	75 g	jam
25 g	50 g	icing sugar
		icing sugar to dredge

1. Preheat the oven to 150 °C/300 °F/gas mark 2.

2. Lightly butter an ovenproof dish.

3. Place the milk, cream and vanilla extract into a saucepan and slowly bring to a gentle boil.

4. In a roomy bowl, whisk the caster sugar with the egg yolks until light and fluffy.

5. Still whisking, slowly add the warmed milk and cream to the egg mixture, taking care not to splash.

6. Finally, add the breadcrumbs and the lemon zest.

7. Place the jam in the bottom of the dish then pour in the egg and breadcrumb mixture.

8. Bake the pudding in the oven for 15–20 minutes or until the mixture is risen and almost set yet still slightly wobbly.

9. In a large, clean roomy bowl, whisk the egg whites until stiff peaks are formed.

10. Whisk in the icing sugar in stages.

11. Remove the pudding from the oven and leave to cool.

12. Raise the oven to 190 °C/375 °F/gas mark 5.

13. Decorate the pudding with a thick layer of meringue.

14. Sprinkle liberally with icing sugar, place in the hot oven and bake for 10 minutes or until the surface is crisp and lightly browned.

Key cookery processes and techniques
Buttering/boiling/whisking/pouring in/baking/browning

Tips
Save some of the jam and mix it through the meringue at the last minute to give a different colour and flavour to it.

Alternative ways in which to enhance the dish
Use all milk instead of the double cream. Pipe on the meringue to give a neat finish.

Ideas for garnishing
Serve with a fresh fruit coulis to complement this dish.

Links to the content of following courses
Hospitality Practical Cookery Int2/Hospitality Skills for Work Int2/Hospitality General Operations Int2

Energy	370 kcal
Fat	17.53 g / 9.57 g saturated
Carbohydrate	50.0 g / 41.13 g sugar
Protein	6.7 g
Fibre	0.3 g

7 St Clementine bakewell

Preparation and cooking time – 55 minutes

2 portions	4 portions	Ingredients
37.5 g	75 g	plain flour
pinch		salt
20 g	40 g	hard margarine
7.5 ml	15 ml	cold water
25 g	50 g	soft margarine
25 g	50 g	caster sugar
25 g	50 g	plain flour
½	1	egg
5 ml	10 ml	lemon marmalade
5 ml	10 ml	orange marmalade
		icing sugar, to dredge

1. Preheat the oven to 200 °C/400 °F/gas mark 6.

2. Sieve the larger quantity of flour and salt into a large bowl.

3. Rub in the margarine until the mixture resembles breadcrumbs.

4. Make a well in the centre, add some of the water and mix to form a firm dough.

5. Knead lightly, cover and allow to rest for 10 minutes until the pastry is required.

6. Beat the soft margarine, caster sugar, smaller quantity of flour and egg in a large bowl until smooth and glossy.

7. Roll the pastry, line a ring and trim.

8. Leave to rest for 5 minutes then bake blind for approximately 10 minutes.

9. Reduce the oven temperature to 180 °C/360 °F/gas mark 4.

10. Spread the marmalades over the base of the pastry case.

11. Spread the sponge mixture over the marmalade.

12. Bake in the oven for 20 minutes until risen and golden brown.

13. Dredge with icing sugar and serve.

Key cookery processes and techniques
Sieving/rubbing in/kneading/beating/rolling/lining/baking blind/baking

Tips
If making 2 portions, it's better to use individual moulds. For 4 portions, the pastry is sufficient for a 15 cm ring.

Alternative ways in which to enhance the dish
Brush the cooked tart with melted marmalade or raspberry jam to glaze the dish.

Ideas for garnishing
Caramelised oranges and mint tips to garnish.

Links to the content of following courses
Hospitality Practical Cookery Int1/Hospitality Skills for Work Int1/Home Economics Standard Grade

Energy	333 kcal
Fat	17.64 g / 6.04 g saturated
Carbohydrate	41.1 g / 17.33 g sugar
Protein	4.9 g
Fibre	1.0 g

 Caramel rice pudding

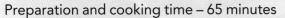

Preparation and cooking time – 65 minutes

2 portions	4 portions	Ingredients
80 g	160 g	short grain rice
600 ml	1.2 l	milk
10 g	20 g	brown sugar
50 g	100 g	caster sugar
60 ml	120 ml	water
Knob		butter

1. Preheat the oven to 150 °C/300 °F/gas mark 2 and grease a 7.5 cm/3 inch deep ovenproof dish.

2. Place the rice, milk and brown sugar in a pan, bring to the boil and simmer for 10 minutes.

3. Meanwhile, put the caster sugar and water in another small pan, bring to the boil and stir carefully.

4. Continue to boil until the mixture starts to change colour. Be very careful not to burn it: as soon as it starts to take on an amber colour, quickly remove it from the heat as it will continue to darken.

5. Stir the caramel into the rice mixture, add the butter and mix well.

6. Pour into the prepared dish, lay a piece of greased greaseproof paper on the top to prevent over-browning and bake in the oven for 45 minutes.

7. Serve hot.

Key cookery processes and techniques
Boiling/simmering/caramelising/baking

Tips
Use a dry oven cloth when handling the hot pans and removing the dish from the oven.

Alternative ways in which to enhance the dish
Add some chopped dried fruit and a pinch of mixed spice to the mixture to give a complementary flavour.

Ideas for garnishing
Freshly poached pears go well with this dish.

Links to the content of following courses
Hospitality Practical Cookery Int1/Hospitality Skills for Work Int1/Home Economics Standard Grade

Energy	209 kcal
Fat	3.78 g / 2.26 g saturated
Carbohydrate	40.1 g / 22.72 g sugar
Protein	6.4 g
Fibre	0.1 g

9 Warm poached pear with chocolate sauce

Preparation and cooking time – 50 minutes

2 portions	4 portions	Ingredients
2	4	pears
50 g	100 g	caster sugar
½	1	vanilla pod
½	1	lemon, juice only
75 ml	150 ml	single cream
10 g	20 g	butter
15 g	30 g	soft brown sugar
50 g	100 g	plain chocolate, broken into chunks

1. Put the pears in a small deep pan and just cover with water.

2. Remove the pears and add sugar to the water.

3. Heat gently until the sugar dissolves; add the vanilla pod.

4. Cut a thin slice off the bottom of the pears so that they will sit upright in the pan, then remove the core through the base.

5. Peel, leaving the stalks intact, then place the pears upright in the pan with the sugar syrup and lemon juice.

6. Bring to the boil and simmer for 20–25 minutes until tender.

7. Meanwhile, put the cream, butter and brown sugar in another pan and heat gently, stirring until hot.

8. Add the chocolate and mix until the sauce is smooth.

9. Remove the pears with a slotted spoon and absorbent paper and arrange on serving plates. Pour the chocolate sauce over the pears, and serve at once.

Key cookery processes and techniques
Poaching/peeling/boiling/simmering

Tips
If you don't have a small pan and the pears won't stay upright, turn them occasionally to ensure even cooking. The cooking time may vary according to the hardness of the pears.

Alternative ways in which to enhance the dish
Use dried spices to flavour the stock syrup instead of the vanilla pod.

Ideas for garnishing
Piped sweetened cream and toasted almonds are a nice way to finish this dish.

Links to the content of following courses
Hospitality Practical Cookery Int2/Hospitality Skills for Work Int2/Hospitality General Operations Int2

Energy	413 kcal
Fat	18.27 g / 11.36 g saturated
Carbohydrate	63.4 g / 63.14 g sugar
Protein	3.1 g
Fibre	3.6 g

1 Chocolate cake

Preparation and cooking time – 60 minutes

2 portions	4 portions	Ingredients
50 g	100 g	soft margarine
50 g	100 g	caster sugar
10 ml	20 ml	water
1	2	eggs
50 g	100 g	self-raising flour
10 ml	20 ml	cocoa
50 ml	100 ml	whipping cream
dash		vanilla essence
10 g	20 g	icing sugar

1. Preheat the oven to 180 °C/360 °F/gas mark 4.

2. Carefully brush the insides of two baking tins with oil.

3. Cream the margarine and caster sugar in a baking bowl until the mixture is light and fluffy. Add water and mix well.

4. Beat the egg in a small bowl.

5. Sift together the flour and the cocoa.

6. Add the egg and flour gradually to the margarine and sugar, mixing well after each addition.

7. Spoon the mixture into the baking tins (same amount in each). Spread out using a knife.

8. Place the baking tins onto a baking tray, place in the oven and bake for 20–25 minutes.

9. When ready, remove the cakes from the tins and cool on a cooling tray.

10. Whip cream to a soft peak and add the vanilla essence and icing sugar.

11. Use the cream mixture to sandwich the sponges together.

Key cookery processes and techniques
Creaming/beating/sifting/mixing/baking/whipping

Tips
When ready the sponges should be springy to the touch. This dish works well when prepared over two days.

Alternative ways in which to enhance the dish
Oranges or black cherries make an additional complement to the basic chocolate sponge.

Ideas for garnishing
Garnish with oranges or black cherries; a chocolate sauce and cocoa powder is another suggestion.

Links to the content of following courses
Hospitality Practical Cookery Int1/Hospitality Skills for Work Int1/Home Economics Standard Grade

Energy	537 kcal
Fat	34.72 g / 14.74 g saturated
Carbohydrate	51.9 g / 32.69 g sugar
Protein	7.5 g
Fibre	1.4 g

Banana bread

Preparation and cooking time – 90 minutes

2 portions	4 portions	Ingredients
125 g	250 g	caster sugar
15 ml	30 ml	water
125 g	250 g	banana flesh
5 ml	10 ml	vanilla essence
50 ml	100 ml	vegetable oil
25 g	50 g	butter
1	2	eggs
25 ml	50 ml	plain yoghurt
75 g	150 g	plain flour
40 g	80 g	wholemeal flour
5 ml	10 ml	mixed spice
1 tsp	2 tsp	baking powder
¼ tsp	½ tsp	bicarbonate of soda

1. Preheat the oven to 175 °C/350 °F/gas mark 4.

2. Butter a mould and line the base with non-stick baking paper.

3. Cook two-thirds of the sugar in a pan with the water until it turns to a dark red caramel.

4. Chop up the banana and add this to the pan along with the vanilla essence.

5. Continue cooking until the banana breaks down and the mixture thickens.

6. Remove from the pan and allow to cool.

7. Beat the remaining sugar with the oil, butter and egg until thick.

8. Add the cooled banana mixture and yoghurt.

9. Sift the remaining ingredients together and fold through the mixture.

10. Spoon into the mould and bake for 35–50 minutes or until cooked.

Key cookery processes and techniques
Chopping/beating/folding/sifting

Tips
Add the bran from the wholemeal flour that remains in the sieve to the mixture. Save time by making the banana mixture in advance.

Alternative ways in which to enhance the dish
Use all butter instead of the oil to give a richer cake. Add chopped nuts to give the cake texture.

Ideas for garnishing
Dust liberally with a mixture of icing sugar and spices. Serve warm with some marscapone.

Links to the content of following courses
Hospitality Practical Cookery Int2/Hospitality Skills for Work Int2/Hospitality General Operations Int2

Energy	868 kcal
Fat	39.88 g / 10.69 g saturated
Carbohydrate	123.8 g / 80.63 g sugar
Protein	11.6 g
Fibre	3.7 g

3 Sticky toffee pudding

Preparation and cooking time – 60 minutes

2 portions	4 portions	Ingredients
125 g	250 g	dates, chopped
85 g	170 g	muscovado sugar
25 g	50 g	butter
½	1	egg
85 g	170 g	plain flour
¼ tsp	½ tsp	bicarbonate of soda
60 g	120 g	dark brown sugar
60 ml	120 ml	single cream
dash		vanilla essence
25 g	50 g	unsalted butter

1. Preheat the oven to 180 °C/360 °F/gas mark 4.

2. Put the dates in a pan and barely cover them with cold water, add the muscovado sugar and butter; bring to the boil and simmer slowly for 8 minutes, then allow to cool.

3. Beat in the egg, flour and bicarbonate of soda. Adjust to a dropping consistency with a little water if required.

4. Spoon the mixture into a well-buttered mould to no more than two-third's full and bake in the oven for 25–30 minutes.

5. Boil the dark brown sugar, single cream, vanilla essence and unsalted butter until slightly thickened.

6. Pour over the sponge while still hot, allow to soak in and serve.

Energy	852 kcal
Fat	28.65 g / 17.53 g saturated
Carbohydrate	150.7 g / 118.28 g sugar
Protein	9.3 g
Fibre	3.8 g

Key cookery processes and techniques
Boiling/simmering/beating/baking

Tips
The boiling of the date mixture can be done in advance, cutting down the time waiting for it to cool before adding the egg.

Alternative ways in which to enhance the dish
Nuts of your choice can be added to the sponge or sauce to give a different taste and texture.

Ideas for garnishing
Vanilla ice cream or sauce complements this dish well.

Links to the content of following courses
Hospitality Practical Cookery Int1/Hospitality Skills for Work Int1/Home Economics Standard Grade

Strawberry and chocolate meringue roulade

Preparation and cooking time – 45 minutes

2 portions	4 portions	Ingredients
2	4	egg whites
100 g	200 g	caster sugar
75 ml	150 ml	whipping cream
10 g	20 g	icing sugar
5	10	strawberries, ripe
25 g	50 g	plain chocolate

1. Preheat the oven to 180 °C/360 °F/gas mark 4.

2. Line a Swiss roll tin with baking paper.

3. Whisk the egg whites until stiff then gradually add the caster sugar until the mixture is thick and glossy.

4. Spoon the meringue mixture into the Swiss roll tin and spread out evenly.

5. Bake in the oven for about 15 minutes. When the meringue is crisp and lightly brown, remove from the oven and allow to cool.

6. Whip the cream until thick then sweeten with the icing sugar.

7. Dice the strawberries and reserve.

8. Melt the chocolate in a bowl slowly over warm water.

9. Lay a fresh piece of greaseproof out on the worktop and dust with caster sugar.

10. Turn the meringue out onto this and remove the baking paper.

11. Spread on the melted chocolate followed by the cream then add the diced strawberries.

12. Roll the roulade up as tightly but gently as possible – it may crack.

13. Dust with icing sugar and serve.

Key cookery processes and techniques
Whisking/spreading/baking/whipping/dicing

Tips
Don't overheat the chocolate as it won't melt to a smooth texture.

Alternative ways in which to enhance the dish
Other fruits can be used such as mango, passion fruit or oranges.

Ideas for garnishing
Serve with chocolate sauce or some fruits.

Links to the content of following courses
Hospitality Practical Cookery Int1/Hospitality Skills for Work Int1/Home Economics Standard Grade

Energy	443 kcal
Fat	18.64 g / 11.56 g saturated
Carbohydrate	68.6 g / 68.4 g sugar
Protein	4.5 g
Fibre	0.7 g

5 Carrot cake

Preparation and cooking time – 80 minutes

2 portions	4 portions	Ingredients
70 g	140 g	carrots, peeled
50 g	100 g	butter
62.5 g	125 g	soft brown sugar
1	2	eggs
2.5 ml	5 ml	ground cinnamon
pinch		ground cardamom
1.25 ml	2.5 ml	mixed spice
85 g	170 g	flour
1 tsp	2 tsp	baking powder
¼	½	lemon, zest and juice
50 g	100 g	ground almonds
62.5 g	125 g	cream cheese
25 g	50 g	icing sugar

1. Preheat the oven to 180 °C/360 °F/gas mark 4.

2. Lightly oil and line a cake tin.

3. Grate the carrots finely.

4. Cream together the butter and brown sugar until pale in colour.

5. Beat the eggs and add gradually to the creamed mixture, beating well each time.

6. Sift the spices, flour and baking powder together then fold into the creamed mixture.

7. Stir in the carrots, lemon zest and juice, and almonds.

8. Put the mixture into the prepared tin, ensuring that the surface is even.

9. Bake for 1 hour, or until cooked.

10. Stir together the cream cheese and icing sugar.

11. When cake is cool, spread mixture on evenly.

Key cookery processes and techniques
Grating/creaming/beating/sifting/baking/stirring

Tips
Weigh ingredients the previous day, which will allow ample time to cook the cake.

Alternative ways in which to enhance the dish
Ginger goes well with carrot; try using this instead of cinnamon.

Ideas for garnishing
Use chopped or half walnuts to finish the cake off. This gives a good complementary flavour.

Links to the content of following courses
Hospitality Practical Cookery Int1/Hospitality Skills for Work Int1/Home Economics Standard Grade

Energy	844 kcal
Fat	53.34 g / 24.49 g saturated
Carbohydrate	83.3 g / 49.18 g sugar
Protein	14.8 g
Fibre	4.0 g

6 Chocolate brownies

Preparation and cooking time – 50 minutes

2 portions	4 portions	Ingredients
		butter for greasing
30 g	60 g	plain chocolate
20 g	40 g	unsalted butter
20 g	40 g	self-raising flour
55 g	110 g	caster sugar
½	1	egg, beaten
1.25 ml	2.5 ml	vanilla essence
12.5 g	25 g	hazelnuts, skinned, roasted and chopped

1. Preheat the oven to 180 °C/360 °F/gas mark 4.

2. Grease a baking tin and line with baking paper.

3. Melt the chocolate and unsalted butter over a bain-marie until lukewarm.

4. Sieve the flour and the sugar together.

5. Stir the egg and vanilla essence into the chocolate mixture and mix well.

6. Fold in the flour and sugar and stir quickly and lightly until smooth.

7. Fold in the nuts.

8. Pour the mixture into the prepared tin and bake for 35 minutes until the top edges are crusty and the inside is gooey but not runny.

9. Leave until lukewarm before cutting.

Key cookery processes and techniques
Melting/sieving/stirring in/folding in/baking

Tips
Use a warmed knife to cut the brownies, cleaning it between each use to give a neat finish.

Alternative ways in which to enhance the dish
Adding chopped nuts will give additional texture and flavour.

Ideas for garnishing
Serve with pouring cream or vanilla ice cream.

Links to the content of following courses
Hospitality Practical Cookery Int1/Hospitality Skills for Work Int1/Home Economics Standard Grade

Energy	365 kcal
Fat	19.22 g / 9.36 g saturated
Carbohydrate	46.3 g / 38.65 g sugar
Protein	4.5 g
Fibre	1.1 g

7 Strawberry shortbreads

Preparation and cooking time – 90 minutes

2 portions	4 portions	Ingredients
75 g	150 g	plain flour
25 g	50 g	pinhead oatmeal
50 g	100 g	butter
25 g	50 g	caster sugar
½	1	egg
75 ml	150 ml	whipping cream
7.5 g	15 g	icing sugar
dash		vanilla essence
4	8	strawberries, ripe

1. Preheat the oven to 180 °C/360 °F/gas mark 4.

2. Sieve the flour into a bowl and add the oatmeal.

3. Rub in the butter until the mixture is a sandy texture.

4. In another bowl mix the egg and sugar.

5. Add to the dry mixture and bind gently to a smooth paste.

6. Leave to rest in the refrigerator for half an hour.

7. Roll out to 2.5 mm thickness and cut into 9 cm rounds.

8. Bake for 10–15 minutes until golden then cool on a rack.

9. Whip the cream and sweeten with the icing sugar and vanilla essence.

10. Cut the strawberries in half or quarter them depending on their size.

11. When the biscuits are cold, pipe the cream on to half of them then assemble the cut strawberries around the outside of the cream.

12. Place the other biscuit on top, dust with icing sugar and serve.

Key cookery processes and techniques
Sieving/rubbing/rolling/baking/whipping/piping

Tips
Make the shortbread in advance to cut down on the time needed to finish this dish. Remove the cooked biscuits from the baking tray with a fish slice so there is less chance of them breaking as they will be fragile.

Alternative ways in which to enhance the dish
Any soft fruit can be used in place of the strawberries if they are not in season.

Ideas for garnishing
A berry coulis or mint syrup would go well with this dish.

Links to the content of following courses
Hospitality Practical Cookery Int2/Hospitality Skills for Work Int2/Hospitality General Operations Int2

Energy	599 kcal
Fat	38.92 g / 23.0 g saturated
Carbohydrate	58.0 g / 20.24 g sugar
Protein	8.1 g
Fibre	2.3 g

Apple strudel

Preparation and cooking time – 90 minutes

2 portions	4 portions	Ingredients
300 g	600 g	eating apples
¼	½	lemon
45 g	90 g	caster sugar
2.5 ml	5 ml	ground cinnamon
20 g	40 g	raisins
3	6	filo pastry sheets, each about 47.5 x 30 cm
25 g	50 g	butter, melted and cooled until tepid
15 ml	30 ml	breadcrumbs, dry
		icing sugar for dusting

Energy	412 kcal
Fat	11.85 g / 6.65 g saturated
Carbohydrate	77.7 g / 49.55 g sugar
Protein	5.5 g
Fibre	4.0 g

1. Preheat the oven to 190 °C/375 °F/gas mark 5.

2. Peel, core and dice the apples. Mix together with the caster sugar, cinnamon and raisins.

3. Lay a large (dry) sheet of greaseproof paper on the work surface.

4. Take one sheet of filo pastry and lay it out flat on greaseproof paper.

5. Brush with melted butter.

6. Take the next sheet; lay it out flat, overlapping the first along the long edge by about 7.5 cm.

7. Brush with the butter.

8. The third sheet is laid exactly over the first, then brushed with butter. If making four portions, the fourth is placed over the second, then brushed with butter, and so on until all the pastry is used up.

9. Sprinkle the dry breadcrumbs over the top two-thirds of the filo pastry, leaving a 4 cm border.

10. Spoon the apple mixture over the breadcrumbs and smooth down lightly.

11. Flip the 4 cm of bare edge over the filling.

12. Now, starting at the top, roll up the pastry round the apple filling, using the greaseproof paper to help you.

13. Carefully lift on to a greased baking tray and curve around into a horseshoe shape.

14. Brush the top with any remaining butter.

15. Bake in the oven for 30–40 minutes, until lightly browned and crisp.

16. Poke a skewer into the centre of the strudel to see if the apple is tender.

17. Loosen the strudel with a knife, then slide carefully on to a serving dish, dust with icing sugar and serve.

Key cookery processes and techniques
Peeling/coring/dicing/mixing/brushing/filling/baking

Tips
To prevent the filo pastry drying out, lay it out, cover with a sheet of greaseproof paper and cover that with a damp tea towel.

Alternative ways in which to enhance the dish
Sprinkle chopped nuts on top of the strudel prior to baking it to give a nice finish and flavour to the dish.

Ideas for garnishing
Serve with hot cream.

Links to the content of following courses
Hospitality Practical Cookery Int2/Hospitality Skills for Work Int2/Hospitality General Operations Int2

9 Apricot and ginger toffee pudding

Preparation and cooking time – 90 to 120 minutes

2 portions	4 portions	Ingredients
30 g	60 g	caster sugar
20 g	40 g	butter
½	1	egg
25 g	50 g	apricots, dried
50 g	100 g	self-raising flour – half white, half brown
⅛ tsp	¼ tsp	bicarbonate of soda
50 ml	100 ml	boiling water
dash		vanilla essence
pinch		ground ginger

1. Preheat the oven to 190 °C/375 °F/gas mark 5.

2. Cream together the caster sugar and the butter until fluffy.

3. Beat the egg and add slowly to the mixture.

4. In a separate bowl, coat the apricots with a little of the flour, add the bicarbonate of soda and the boiling water.

5. Add the rest of the flour, vanilla essence and ginger to the butter/sugar/egg mixture.

6. Add the apricot mixture.

7. Turn the mixture into a suitably sized tray and bake 1–1½ hours depending on the quantity you're making.

8. The cake is ready when a knife comes out clean from the centre.

Key cookery processes and techniques
Creaming/beating/baking

Tips
Weighing ingredients before starting will allow for the techniques and cooking to be undertaken in one lesson.

Alternative ways in which to enhance the dish
Add some stem ginger to give a stronger flavour to the dish.

Ideas for garnishing
Serve with a thin toffee sauce, using some of it to coat the sponge when it comes out of the oven first.

Links to the content of following courses
Hospitality Practical Cookery Int1/Hospitality Skills for Work Int1/Home Economics Standard Grade

Energy	256 kcal
Fat	10.36 g / 5.75 g saturated
Carbohydrate	38.0 g / 20.85 g sugar
Protein	5.2 g
Fibre	2.3 g

Time plan 1

This time plan is an example of how planning could be carried out for a two-dish, 1½ hour practical session using the following recipes:

Smoked bacon melts   P33
Leek flan   P71

Times	Sequence of tasks
0–10 minutes	Set oven, make pastry.
10–20 minutes	Cut all vegetables and bacon.
20–30 minutes	Make mixture for melts.
30–35 minutes	Line flan and bake blind for 20 minutes.
35–45 minutes	Make flan filling, preheat grill.
45–55 minutes	Toast bread and grate cheese.
55–60 minutes	Add filling to flan, bake for 15 minutes.
60–75 minutes	Finish melts and serve.
75–90 minutes	Remove flan from oven and serve. Tidy down.

Time plan 2

This time plan is an example of how planning could be carried out for a three-dish, 2½ hour practical session using the following recipes:

Butternut squash soup   P39
Chicken burger with relish   P56
Chocolate tart   P92

Times	Sequence of tasks
0–10 minutes	Turn on oven and make pastry.
10–25 minutes	Prepare vegetables.
25–35 minutes	Roll out pastry.
35–50 minutes	Make burgers.
50–55 minutes	Bake pastry blind.
55–70 minutes	Make relish.
70–75 minutes	Remove baking beans, continue cooking for 5 minutes then reduce oven temp.
75–80 minutes	Melt chocolate, make chocolate filling and brush flan.
80–85 minutes	Fill and bake tarts.
85–100 minutes	Finish soup and blend.
100–110 minutes	Tidy down work area.
110–115 minutes	Turn on grill. Reheat soup, season and serve.
115–130 minutes	Grill burgers and warm buns.
130–140 minutes	Serve burgers.
140–150 minutes	Serve tart and tidy down.